POSITIVELY
GARCIA

REFLECTIONS OF THE JGB
HOWARD F. WEINER

ISBN: 1499215606
ISBN 13: 9781499215601

Pencil Hill Publishing New York, New York

Contents

REFLECTIONS OF THE JGB

APPENDIX

"There's no way to measure his greatness or magnitude as a person or as a player. I don't think any eulogizing will do him justice. He was that great, much more than a superb musician, with an uncanny ear and dexterity. He's the very spirit personified of whatever is Muddy River country at its core and screams up into the spheres. He really had no equal. To me he wasn't only a musician and friend, he was more like a big brother who taught and showed me more than he'll ever know. There's a lot of spaces and advances between The Carter Family, Buddy Holly and, say, Ornette Coleman—a lot of universes, but he filled them all without being a member of any school. His playing was moody, awesome, sophisticated, hypnotic and subtle. There's no way to convey the loss. It just digs down really deep."

- Bob Dylan on the passing of Jerry Garcia, 1995.

PRELUDE

THE ANNALS OF
JGB OBSESSION

A panel of top guitarists and "other experts" were assembled to rank the 100 greatest guitarists for a special issue of *Rolling Stone* in 2011. It came as no revelation that Jimi Hendrix was once again crowned king of the guitar universe, with Eric Clapton, Jimmy Page, Keith Richards, and Jeff Beck rounding out the top five spots, in that order. The man that I rank as the greatest guitarist, Jerry Garcia, landed in the forty-sixth spot on this *Rolling Stone* list of virtuosos. This absurd ranking irks me, but it's not surprising. During his thirty years as the legendary leader of the Grateful Dead, Garcia was the most bootlegged and prolific guitarist of his time. Almost all of the band's 2,318 concerts were recorded by dedicated tapers, and they're still being devoured, dissected and discussed by hundreds of thousands of Deadheads decades after Garcia's death. In addition to this live canon, Garcia consistently toured with his own band, and in the process, created another treasure trove of live music. So what gives? Why is one of the most talented, innovative, and influential artists of his time so vastly underrated?

Early in their career, the Grateful Dead blew monumental opportunities to advance their popularity and legacy. While Hendrix immortalized himself with sensational performances at the Woodstock and Monterey festivals, the Grateful Dead refused to allow footage of their performance to be used in either film. It was a foolish business decision, even though their set at Woodstock was subpar and fraught with weirdness. After Woodstock, the band finally recorded two excellent albums, *Workingman's Dead* and *American Beauty*, but neither album captured the essence of a Grateful Dead concert, or showcased the improvisational genius of their lead guitar player.

Critics and fans alike tend to judge musical artists by their discographies, and based strictly on that criteria, I can understand how Garcia was not perceived as an elite top-ten guitarist. However, after "Touch of Grey," the Grateful Dead's first hit and MTV video, the band's popularity grew exponentially at the end of the 1980s. In the early '90s, the band began to officially release concerts from their vault. Most notably there was Dick's Picks, CD releases of shows selected by Grateful Dead archivist Dick Latvala. This scintillating series shines a luminous light on the band, and the talents of Garcia, but it was too much, too late. Outside of their targeted fan base, there's little commercial or critical interest in concerts from decades past. The genius of Hendrix, Santana, or Clapton is easily accessible in defining albums such as *The Jimi Hendrix Experience*, *Electric Ladyland*, *Abraxas*, *Wheels of Fire*, and *Layla and other Assorted Love Songs*. There are few common denominators in Garcia's oeuvre. If one enters the Library of Garcia, the archives are overstocked with inspirational nuggets, yet the defining masterpieces are scarce. If you ask 300 Deadheads what album or performance best portrays the essence of Garcia, you'll get 250 different answers.

Tackling Garcia's output as a performing artist is an impossible task for one author. There are three volumes of *The Deadhead's Taping Compendium*, in which a sizeable team of reviewers chronicle thirty years' worth of Grateful Dead performances over the span of 2,216 pages. The last of these informative and cumbersome compendiums came out in 2000. Since then, an abundance of new and improved recordings have surfaced, thanks to the proliferation of music via the Internet.

These new recordings alone could justify a fourth volume in the compendium series. There's never-ending Cyberspace chatter on a plethora of websites about the minutia of Grateful Dead gigs from all eras. Even *Rolling Stone* got in on the act as David Fricke recently offered up a list of twenty essential Grateful Dead shows. Music nerds love lists, even if they agitate us because they stoke the critic within. Every time *Rolling Stone* unleashes a greatest albums list, I dust off my *Sergeant Pepper's Lonely Hearts Club Band* and *Pet Sounds* CDs, and try to figure out how anyone could rank these ahead of Dylan's *Highway 61 Revisited.* *Sergeant Pepper's Lonely Hearts Club Band* isn't a top five Beatles album, and I've never conversed with anybody who thinks that *Pet Sounds* is the second-greatest album ever.

As for Mr. Fricke's essential Grateful Dead list, he only includes one show from 1977-1983, yet his list includes four shows from 1987-1991, a much weaker era in live Dead history. Fricke's concert descriptions don't reflect the expertise of one who has given up decades of his life to obsess over Garcia's every solo, but the list sparked a spirited conversation amongst Deadheads. Around the same time as Fricke's piece, *The New Yorker* featured an article titled "Annals Of Obsession: Deadhead, The Afterlife," penned by Nick Paumgarten. This is one of the most compelling articles I've ever read about the musical culture of the Grateful Dead. Spurred on by Paumgarten and Fricke, I desired to write a book on the band's music that revolved around some kind of list. After kicking that notion around for a few days, I realized that working on that type of book might be like beating on a Dead Horse. In that moment of lucidity, the inspiration I was seeking mysteriously appeared, as if my mission was predestined.

As far as I knew, nobody had yet to write a book on the Jerry Garcia Band. There are no memoirs, compendiums, chronicles, or essay collections that pertain exclusively to this topic. From 1968 through 1995, Garcia appeared 1,664 times without the Grateful Dead, and a large portion of those shows were with the Jerry Garcia Band. They didn't go by the JGB moniker until 1975, but essentially, Garcia Band began in 1970, when he first gigged in small California clubs with John Kahn, Merl Saunders, and Bill Vitt. If the Grateful Dead were the most consistent, innovative, and beloved touring band of their time, then the Jerry Garcia Band would arguably be the second-best touring band in the land during that era. When the Grateful Dead were on the lam, a Deadhead could always count on a JGB jam. The Garcia never stopped. Somewhat lost in the annals of Grateful Dead obsession is the astonishing productivity of JGB.

My first instinct was to rank the fifty best Jerry Garcia Band shows, then pontificate upon each show for a few pages. But how does a critic justify that show number forty-three is better than show twenty-six? With any list that extends to fifty or a hundred, there's a huge safety net; no tough choices or cuts are being made. And besides, I really wanted to examine the best of the best, and spend time inside the belly of the beast exploring what really made Garcia tick. I hoped to find something extraordinary and transcendent within every performance I'd write about. After jotting down forty or fifty best show candidates, I decided that a dozen dazzling performances would do. There would be nothing disingenuous or overhyped on this list. These shows had to reflect the diversity of the Zen alchemist, Jerry Garcia. After gorging myself on JGB bootlegs for the past thirty years, I was ready to get down to the nitty-gritty.

As I began to separate the wheat from the chaff, there existed a great divide. Almost all of my best-show candidates were from a twelve-year span, 1972 through 1984, the years when Garcia's guitar prowess was unfettered. Due primarily to Garcia's health issues, JGB cut back on their touring schedule in 1985, and prior to the heart-wrenching coma that befell Jerry after a Dead show in Washington, DC in the summer of '86, Garcia had only toured acoustically with John Kahn that year. Much to the delight of Deadhead Nation, Garcia was back in action with JGB two months after the nearly fatal coma. The bad news was that he had to relearn how to play guitar. During his comeback, Garcia proved he was still a shaman capable of delivering euphoria to adoring crowds through his poignant style; but something was amiss. His solos weren't as imaginative or tenacious as before. The thrill was still there, but Garcia was changing as an artist. In JGB's live rotation, songs showcasing major jams like "Sugaree," "Catfish John," "Rhapsody In Red," "Mystery Train," and "That's All Right Mama," were replaced by lighter fare such as "Evangeline," "My Sisters and Brothers," "Lay Down Sally," and "Waiting For a Miracle." JGB shows took on a spiritual tone. Soothing gospel harmonies gradually replaced the propulsion of hardcore blues and rock and roll.

Acoustic studio collaborations with David Grisman and Tony Rice were amongst the most compelling works of Garcia's later career. Any worthwhile retrospective of Garcia in the '90s would require a balanced study of his live and studio performances. Garcia released six albums during the years I'm writing about. With the exception of the vague and timid *Run For the Roses*, the other albums were respectable efforts that failed to set off any record buying frenzies. For the most part, these albums contained sketches and snapshots of songs that exploded like Roman candles when JGB expanded and transformed them in concert. Remastered versions of these albums comprise the *All Good Things: Jerry Garcia Studio Sessions* box set which also features a bonanza of gratifying bonus tracks. Since I was seeking twelve immortal JGB performances that would define Garcia as an artist, I went fishing where the pond was stocked. I opened up the coffers of my live Garcia archive, which contains over 1,000 CDs, and immersed myself in the golden years, 1972 through 1984.

While working on this Garcia project, I liberated myself from the trappings of Grateful Dead mythology. Don't get me wrong, everybody loves reading about the mystical rise of the Grateful Dead: the Electric Kool-Aid Acid Tests, the Merry Pranksters, Ken Kesey, Neal Cassady, Mountain Girl, Owsley's LSD and theories on sound, how the Grateful Dead survived on nothing but acid, red meat and rock and roll in L.A., the Haight-Ashbury scene, communal living on 710 Fulton Street, free concerts in Golden Gate Park, Bill Graham, Rock Scully, Hell's Angels,

Ramrod, the Carousel Ballroom, the Fillmores (East and West), the busts in San Francisco and New Orleans...on and on it went, and somewhere, lost in the midst of it all, was the inspirational lightening rod for the whole scene, Captain Trips, Jerry Garcia. Do you think Jimi Hendrix, Jimmy Page, or Jim Morrison had to compete with such external ruckus? Garcia was in the thick of a psychedelic dream, a fabled wonderland; but all the hoopla did little to advance his reputation as a masterful musician, although Captain Trips was light years away from contemplating his legacy.

There's almost no folklore attached to the Jerry Garcia Band; any mythology they have falls under the Grateful Dead umbrella. For JGB, it was all about the music, no hassles. Oh, how Jerry hated hassles or confrontations of any ilk. The slender, and supremely talented chain-smoking San Francisco bassist, John Kahn, was Garcia's trusted confidante, and a lifetime JGB member. Garcia rolled with an unpretentious crew. Fancy boys need not apply. Night after night, Garcia and Kahn keenly played music for music's sake. They performed for gatherings of hedonistic Deadheads in small venues. The Grateful Dead journey was a long, strange communal trip across arcane terrain. Following the Jerry Garcia Band was for the privileged few, a musical orgy for those in the know, especially in those early years.

Since I first discovered the joys of JGB, I've developed a resolute fondness for certain shows, but my final list ended up surprising me. 2-17-80 Oswego and 11-4-81 Albany, early long shots to make the list, ended up in the fourth and sixth spots respectively after I closely listened to the top contenders. I didn't think an acoustic gig could crack the top twelve, but 5-5-82 Oregon State Penitentiary ended up in the eighth spot; that was Garcia and Kahn's *Live At Folsom Prison*. My list of twelve turned into a baker's dozen when I discovered 8-20-81 Keystone Berkeley, right before I was finalizing my selections. I made room for 8-20-81 by moving it into a twelfth-place tie with 2-5-81 Lehigh. I refer to these shows by their numerical dates because that's the common lingo amongst Deadheads and Garcia aficionados. Mention 5-8-77 to a

Deadhead and listen to him or her give you their opinion on the Grateful Dead show that night from Barton Hall in Cornell. And if somebody tries to tell you that show is overrated, don't believe it. These numerical dates are sacred, since they've become the de facto titles of Garcia's greatest music. Rolling Stones fans have *Beggar's Banquet, Sticky Fingers,* and *Exile on Main Street.* Deadheads have 9-21-72 Philly Spectrum, 6-16-74 Des Moines, and 9-3-77 Englishtown.

As I amassed this collection of elite performances, I steered free of political correctness. I would have liked to pay homage to all the great musicians who played with Garcia through these years, but I trusted my discerning tastes and picked Garcia's finest performances, and in the process, two fabulous JGB configurations are not represented. In 1975, one of the most revered piano players of the rock era, Nicky Hopkins, joined forces with Garcia for a couple of months. Hearing these maestros side by side in collaboration is a fantasy realized. A few of these shows were in contention for the final cut of my baker's dozen, but if one would have made it through, it would have been because I wanted to commemorate Nicky Hopkins' time in JGB, not because of the merits of that given show. In 1978, folkie-blues singer, Maria Muldaur joined her boyfriend Kahn, along with Donna and Keith Godchaux, and former Elvis Presley drummer Ron Tutt, in a most impressive JGB configuration. A few of their March shows came close to cracking my dynamic dozen, but Garcia Band was in its prime when either Merl Saunders or Melvin Seals were laying down their sweeping, swishing, soulful organ riffs.

Before they were known as the Jerry Garcia Band, Saunders and Kahn formed the nucleus for Garcia's electric bands through 1975. Three shows from this period made my list, including the lord of them all, 2-6-72 Pacific High Studios. After Melvin Seals replaced Ozzie Ahlers on keyboards towards the end of 1980, JGB had their ideal organ grinder. Seals remained on the bench, behind his Hammond organ, for the next fifteen years. Seven shows with Seals from the years 1981-1983 made the list, as well as two 1980 shows with Ahlers on keyboards.

While the Jerry Garcia Band was steaming through the early '80s, the Grateful Dead stumbled into a creative rut. More than ever, it seemed like the Grateful Dead were going through the motions; they weren't communicating as well on stage, and personal relations were strained off stage. But like a married couple that takes the "for better or worse" vow seriously, the band plowed ahead. As Bill Graham said, "They're not the best at what they do, they're the only ones that do what they do." And somehow, in spite of limited commercial success, and an occasional clunker of a show, the band still thrilled their zealous followers. Deadhead Nation was on the rise and stronger than ever. However, these were extremely dark days for Garcia, who cut himself off from the world and found solace in smoking Persian, a highly addictive and refined Iranian opium that will eventually rob you of your dignity. Besides scoring dope, Garcia's other passion was jamming in a hassle-free zone, and rolling with JGB was much easier than hitting the road with the Grateful Dead juggernaut.

Garcia gigs throughout the '70s were idiosyncratic affairs, featuring Jerry sharing his muse in an unpretentious manner. During this same time period, the Grateful Dead shattered sonic barriers on stage with their surging, transcendent jams. However, there was no comparison between the two. A Grateful Dead concert was a longer, weirder and wilder ride than a JGB show. In the early '80s the tide shifted, and the gap between bands narrowed. After years of trial by fire, and tinkering with the sound and line-ups of his bands, Garcia had mastered a reliable rotation of songs, and he had a band that was in sync with his vision. JGB was pumping out thrilling shows that were on par with what the Grateful Dead were doing, and their appearances in modest clubs and exquisite theatres made the JGB experience more intimate.

Garcia played several shows with Old & In the Way in 1973, and the Great American String Band in 1974. In these bluegrass groups, Garcia was an equal contributor, not the dominant force guiding the group, so these performances didn't fall under the JGB umbrella for the purposes of this book. At the end of 1974, Garcia and Saunders put together a band called Legion of Mary. Saunders sang on a song or two, but Garcia was still the focal point and leader of the band. From a strong group of contending Legion of Mary shows, 7-4-75 Great American Music Hall made the fifth spot on my list. In 1979, Garcia and Saunders formed Reconstruction, a jazz-based group. It was an experiment that produced eclectic results, although nothing landed in my top twelve.

The thirteen shows selected for *Positively Garcia* are all bootleg recordings that have yet to be officially released. Four of these shows are soundboards, the other nine are audience recordings. Officially released shows from the Keystone Berkrley (1973), Warner Theatre (1978), and Kean College (1980) were all serious contenders for the list, but it was fitting that my politically incorrect choices were all bootlegs. If JGB played an early and a late show, I rated each show on its own merit. As a result, only one late show and no early shows made the list. It's hard for any performer to let the mojo roll during an early show if there's a late show on the horizon. Conversely, a performer never starts a late show with a full tank, as a certain amount of energy has already been expended.

To help alleviate the confusion brought on by the shuffling personnel in the band, the appendix contains a chronological listing of JGB lineups from 1975-1995. I discovered this list on Corry Arnold's *Lost Live Dead* blog. It's by far the most accurate and updated record of band personnel. There's a lot of conflicting and missing information out there, especially in regards to Garcia's early years outside the Grateful Dead. I put in an honorable effort to get all the facts straight, but ultimately this isn't an official database, these are essays and tales of inspiration.

As I pondered the performances of *Positively Garcia*, a clearer picture of Garcia began to emerge. He was an alchemist with a brilliant ear who drew sonic inspiration from multiple genres. JGB's canon of songs over this twelve-year period is strange and random at first glance; yet, after closer inspection, the songs are cohesive under Garcia's direction. They're peas in a pod, relatives at a family reunion. Due to the improvisational and lengthy nature of Garcia's guitar meanderings, it's easy to think of him as a free spirit who simply played as he pleased. Yet there was great equilibrium and logic in the way he attacked solos and set lists. After ensconcing myself in almost nothing but JGB CDs for a twelve-month stretch, I created a hypothetical box set using the best performances taken from the shows I've critiqued. I've dubbed this hypothetical box set the *Keystone Years Anthology*. Keystone Berkeley was a small, inconspicuous San Francisco night club that was opened for business in 1972, and was shut down in 1984. These years neatly correspond with the time frame of my book. Garcia played the Keystone Berkeley 206 times, way more than any other venue, and the iconic *Live at Keystone* was recorded there in 1973. The very mention of the word Keystone makes Deadheads salivate like Pavlov's dogs.

I classified the songs of the *Keystone Years Anthology* into six categories that comprise six CDs. The first two discs feature the songs of Garcia's main muses, Bob Dylan and Robert Hunter. CD three is a buoyant collage of love ballads, optimistic Jerry at his best. Garcia's virtuosity rages on the fourth disc, *Epic Jams*. On the fifth disc, *Influences*, Garcia digs into his roots and explores indelible songs from the '50s and '60s, tunes that ignited a cultural revolution. On the final disc, *Inspirations*, Garcia applies his golden touch to timeless compositions written by his contemporary peers. Through his patient and passionate interpretations, these songs coalesce into Garcia's diverse vision of the American experience. These tunes seem to speak to each other on a cosmic level. This left Garcia free to pick and choose from any category during the course of a live performance—it all rolls into one.

Touring with the Jerry Garcia Band was an intense experience. In my memoir, *Tangled Up in Tunes: Ballad of a Dylanhead*, I chronicled my life of musical obsession centered around years of touring with the Grateful Dead, the Jerry Garcia Band, and Bob Dylan. I only briefly touched upon my JGB experiences, so I couldn't pass on this chance to stroll down memory lane—*play it again, Sam*. In the second part of this book, Reflections of the JGB, I revisit my early days of wanderlust, a time of innocence when I wildly and blindly pursued my desires.

During my most intensive touring days, which spanned from 1981 to 1984, I had the good fortune of catching thirty-five JGB gigs, and eighty-one Grateful Dead shows. The contrast between the tours was drastic. The Dead tour was a bonding experience—a caravan of stoned strangers coming together out on the road in arcane terrain—the ultimate getaway adventure without brochures or a cruise director. Chasing JGB was an extreme compulsion. Gone were the weird smells, sights, and sounds of Deadheads buzzing around a dirt parking lot in places like East Troy, Wisconsin. Traveling in packs of two or three, most of us Jerry Heads would meet up after work or college classes, drive two hours to see JGB in a quaint place, and then drive back home and do it all over again the next day. This was more of a mission than a vacation. Those of us who followed JGB tended be snobbish connoisseurs, true Jerry Junkies. With some of the shenanigans, hoopla and hype of the Dead tour out of the equation, we were free to immerse ourselves in Pure Jerry.

Garcia's wardrobe and stage demeanor were as humble as could be for rock and roll royalty. The JGB platform gave this egoless superstar the opportunity to live the life he loved in a relatively hassle free environment. After gigs, Garcia and Kahn weren't the type of cats who would charge into an establishment and ignite a barroom brawl. There are no tales of an inebriated Jerry heaving TVs out hotel windows, although Mr. Garcia was infamous for nodding out and leaving behind a smoking trail of burnt carpets and seat cushions that set off a symphony of smoke alarms. However, Garcia's greatest contribution to society is the blazing trail of eternal inspiration that he left behind, and *Positively Garcia* is a slice of that pie. These are the narratives of the shows, the songs, the solos, and the magnificent venues that he played in. The Roseland Ballroom, Cape Cod Coliseum, Music Mountain, Keystone Korner and Keystone Berkeley have all been shut down, but Garcia's performances at these musical shrines immortalize a special time and place in America. Based solely on this twelve-year period in Jerry's solo career, I place Garcia at the top of the greatest guitarist heap. Hopefully

Garcia's legacy will continue to grow, and he'll advance past the forty-sixth spot in the next *Rolling Stone* Greatest Guitarist poll. Regardless, his liberating licks and heartfelt vocals will continue to touch the hearts and minds of millions. Here's to the genius of Garcia's generosity.

POSITIVELY GARCIA

Jerry Garcia at the Calderone Concert Hall, February 29, 1980. ©Jay Blakesberg

1

BUSY BEING BORN

As Garcia, Saunders, Kahn, and Kreutzmann launch "It Takes a Lot to Laugh, It Takes a Train to Cry," time's suspended by the hypnotic groove. It's a Dylan tune, yet there are no lyrics to ponder. The repetitive riff is sublime—Frisco Blues—as mysterious and vast as the Pacific, yet heavenly and cool in the style of Miles. Garcia's snapping strings sing a lonely lullaby—poetry-in motion. The drummer and bassist are locked in tight, and the beat bounces brightly as the earthy vibrations of the Hammond organ swirl in and out and all around—aural ecstasy! This blues riff will never sound this good again, and the musicians know IT. There's a song to be sung, somewhere down the line, but the band proceeds deliberately, intent on basking in the moment. A modest studio gathering and a privileged West Coast FM radio audience are listening in on this intimate musical conversation. Out of the mesmerizing groove, a mellifluous voice suddenly whispers:

"KSAN in San Francisco."

Ordinarily this type of interruption would defile a masterpiece like a scar on the Mona Lisa, but the lady DJ sounds sultry, and it seamlessly intertwines with the music as if it were preordained. And if ever a radio station deserved to beat their chest, KSAN deserved props for broadcasting this jam from Pacific High Studios on 60 Brady Street in San Francisco. The musicians in the studio couldn't hear the radio call letters, but Garcia is seemingly spurred on as if he could hear the DJ's titilating tones. With each round, his leads become more pronounced and provocative. Garcia's obviously an inspired man, possibly possessed. Even the purest of archivists wouldn't wish away the KSAN interruption. It's a stamp of immortality.

Jerry draws a deep breath, steps to the mic, and an angelic voice fills the air. "Wintertime's coming, it's filled with frost. I tried to tell everybody but I could not get across."

Hey, Jerry, wrong verse…wrong lyrics! Garcia sings the third verse instead of the first, and Dylan's words are, "THE WINDOWS are filled with frost." Yet we'll forgive this faux pas because the bearded guru is singing with feeling, sweet and true. Without a trademark solo, Jerry transitions from the third verse to the first:

"I ride a mail train, mama, can't buy a thrill." Priceless. Garcia caresses every syllable until the jingle nimbly touches down. Garcia will perform more complex versions of "It Takes a Lot to Laugh, It Takes a Train to Cry," but few satisfy like this odd nugget which radiates in its own imperfection. If I were commissioned to arrange a soundtrack for a documentary on the essence of Garcia as a performer, this is where it would begin.

The band noodles and doodles in preparation for the next entrée. Garcia has a thing for tuning up. It's an artistic endeavor for him, and quite frankly, the guy's got a problem; he can't stop picking. Someone in the pocket-sized audience yells out a barely audible request, and Garcia replies, "Everything's gonna be all right." Sure, that was easy for Mr. Garcia to say. By 1972, he had the hip world at his command. With the Grateful Dead's most recent vinyl releases, *Workingman's Dead* (recorded in Pacific High Studios) and *American Beauty,* the band had finally tasted commercial success and critical acclaim. The band's lyricist, Robert Hunter, was on the mother of all rolls, penning verse after verse, and anthem after anthem, as if he were Robert Allen Zimmerman, the pen master himself. And the twenty-nine-year-old leader of the band, Jerry Garcia, was a virtuoso in his prime, unleashing visions and dreams beyond imagination. With Kahn, Kreutzmann, and Saunders jamming by his side, Garcia glowed. Everything's gonna be all right, indeed.

Jerry Garcia, 1972 © Philip Gould/CORBIS

Following Garcia's proclamation, the band slams into "Expressway To Your Heart." All aboard the Motown Express! This little ditty penned by Gamble and Huff, and made famous by The Soul Survivors, is now a vehicle bulleting at the speed of sound—a bawdy traveling companion for "It Takes a Train to Cry." Garcia and friends hammer "Expressway" as if this is the last jam of humanity. This tour de force rages down a jagged highway, and the band never eases off the gas—ten minutes of thrills at breakneck speeds. They interact as if they've sped down this road a thousand times before; however, this is their debut gig as a quartet. Jerry defers to Merl a few times, and Saunders drains a whole lotta soul from his Hammond B-3 organ. But on this number, Garcia's driving the train, and it's quite possible he's high on cocaine. His volatile playing veers off the tracks, yet the Bearded One finds his way back home by balancing musical equations on the fly.

For this Pacific High gig, Grateful Dead drummer Billy Kreutzmann, fills in for Bill Vitt, who had handled drumming duties for most of the Garcia/ Saunders shows. The familiarity of having Kreutzmann striking the skins is a rallying force for Garcia, and it energizes the quartet as a whole. The first Garcia/Saunders show took place on December 15, 1970, and after twenty or so performances, Garcia and Saunders were bubbling like lava. Jerry had also been moonlighting with the New Riders of the Purple Sage, but this involvement with Saunders and Kahn had developed into his pet project outside of the Grateful Dead. With Kreutzmann on board, this was perhaps the finest band of Bay Area musicians ever assembled. These visionaries were on the same wavelength, speaking the same language; yet there was virginal excitement in Pacific High Studios—a talented group hitting it off on their first date.

On the heels of such a fanciful Pacific High opening, "That's a Touch I Like" is no slouch in the third slot; in fact, it's ravishing. After a crisp opening solo, Jerry croons, "Red ribbons in your hair, I'm kind of glad that you put them there. That's the touch I like. That's the touch I like. Whoa-oh-oh, that's the touch I like." This snippet of female infatuation was penned by Jesse Winchester for his eponymous 1970 album.

On that record, this tune is mislabeled as "That's *the* Touch I Like," and that's the touch Garcia likes, because that's the way he sings it. Winchester actually sang, "That's *a* touch I like," and when his album was reissued on CD in 2006, the title was corrected.

Anyway, those witnesses at 60 Brady Street must have been swept out of their seats. Garcia's charm and inquisitive nature took center stage. Is it the red ribbon, or the woman, that sparks the singer's imagination? Either way, Jerry's so pleased, he concedes, "I'll be on my very best behavior." The pulse and vibration of this performance is infectious, an instant remedy for the blues.

In arcane ways, these songs seem to be communicating with each other; each tune has a companion. It begins with the traveling tunes, "Train to Cry" and "Expressway." The flipside for "That's a Touch I Like" is this show's encore, "How Sweet It Is." Written by the team of Holland-Dozier-Holland, and popularized by both Marvin Gaye and James Taylor. "How Sweet It Is" would go on to be immortalized by the Jerry Garcia Band, becoming the signature feel-good opener, and the band's most frequently played number. In substance and style, "How Sweet It Is" and "That's a Touch I Like" are siblings; yet, "That's a Touch I Like" would never be performed again after May 21, 1975. Of the two, I prefer Jesse Winchester's baby. It could have been a dynamite alternative opener to the overplayed "How Sweet It Is." However, on this night, both ballads are rapturous, a snapshot of Jerry's giddy optimism.

These were also optimistic times for American culture. In February of 1972, two cinematic classics, *The Godfather* and *Deliverance*, were released, and Don Mclean's "American Pie" was number one on the Billboard charts. In matters of war and peace, these were turbulent times. The United States was fatigued from a decade of civil strife and the horror of the never-ending war in Vietnam. Moving songs of protest, empowerment, and hope were replaced by monumental escapist anthems and Teflon rock. Maybe music couldn't change the world, but it could take you to another time and place—transcendence. And in 1972, nobody was improvising mind-bending guitar jams like Jerome Kearns Garcia.

Back in Pacific High Studios, Kahn kicks off "Save Mother Earth" with thick, brooding bass blasts. Soulful riffs from Saunders ensue, and Garcia answers with yearning guitar bursts. The only original played by the band on this night, "Save Mother Earth" was written by Saunders for his soon-to-be-released album, *Heavy Turbulence*, which would also feature the following number, "Imagine."

Garcia must be donning Superman's cape as he wails on "Save Mother Earth." Captain Trips breaks the instrumental free from the mother ship, spinning and spiraling it to the cosmos and beyond—"Dark Star" > "Mind Left Body Jam" territory, the psychedelic providence of the Grateful Dead. Jerry pecks away frantically and the sonic voyage gets way out there—farther, further, faster. When the exploration crackles, fizzles and fades, Saunders gently leads the band into "Imagine." The audience applauds the soothing familiarity of the melody, relieved to be floating back towards earth. The segue is flawless. There's no attempt to sing Lennon's song. Garcia's guitar humbly and simply pleads for peace on earth.

For Deadheads who collected bootlegs prior to the proliferation of digitized music, "Imagine" is the last song on the first side of a ninety-minute Maxell XLII cassette tape. The tape from 2-6-72 is a perfectly balanced boot that plays like an album. Sides A and B have their own distinctive mojo, and they complement each other as if they are separate sets, although this is a ninety-minute performance with no break. As the most bootlegged performer of his time, Garcia seemingly had a sixth sense for filling up tapes, as if he was performing especially for the tapers. This notion is not farfetched. In the early '60s, Garcia bootlegged largely unknown and wildly talented bluegrass musicians—the very troubadours that fueled Garcia's guitar picking fetish.

Side B commences with "That's All right Mama," a four-solo pressure cooker—Beale Street spirit meets New York City tenacity. *Rolling Stone* magazine identified Elvis Presley's recording of "That's All right

Mama" as the first rock and roll record, and Garcia's extended version embdies and amplifies that rowdy/rebellious swagger. "One and one is two. Two and two is four," sings Jerry. Improvisation is like arithmetic in Garcia's brain. The waterfall of creativity flows from his guitar, yet it all makes sense; every note is a number leading to the final sum. Transparency. When Garcia's in the zone, he's like Einstein on bennies—in front of a blackboard, chalk in hand.

Lingering in the Mississippi Delta, the band pairs "That's All Right Mama" with Jimmie Rodgers' "That's All Right," a song that has been mislabeled on most Pacific High Studio tapes as "Who's Loving You Tonight." The circulating KSAN tape is missing the opening of this song and it's a damned shame, because as we jump in, Garcia's on a rampage; his searing leads sizzle in agony. Saunders leans into his Hammond and unleashes hissing, hell-bent blues, the nasty and tenacious strain. As Jerry follows, he comes off like Clapton, Bloomfield, and Stills all rolled into one, and as he finishes out this tribute he howls, "But now that I wonder, whoo-ooh-ooh-ohh's loving you tonight." Somewhere in heaven, Jimmie Rodgers yodels back his approval.

An iconic album, or performance, is usually characterized by a magnificently orchestrated selection of songs that relate to, and build upon, each other, so that the listener is drawn deeper into the web of the artist's vision. If you hit a shuffle button and randomly listen to the songs of *Abbey Road*, the playback won't create the same experience as if the songs were heard in their rightful order, as consciously conceived by The Beatles and George Martin. The songs still stand on their own, but their collective power diminishes. Great live performances can be consciously orchestrated, but I prefer the thrill of free-flowing improvisational genius, which under the right circumstances, and fueled by the right momentum, can create a masterpiece that exceeds what the performer or audience could have ever imagined. On 2-6-72, Garcia is in that rarified air. After the Jimmie Rodgers' stomp, Garcia paints his masterpiece with Dylan's "When I Paint My Masterpiece."

"Oh, the streets of Rome are filled with rubble, ancient footprints are everywhere," croons Garcia—admiration and awe blatant in his delivery. In Garcia's world, Dylan's visions are glorified: *Inside The Coliseum, dodging lions and wasting time...I landed in Brussels, on a plane ride so bumpy that I almost cried...Train wheels running through the back of my memory...Young men in uniform and young girls pulling mussels...Newspaper man eating candy, had to be held back by big police.* Oh, the sights and sounds! In Dylan's studio recording of "When I Paint My Masterpiece," the kaleidoscope of images are stacked upon each other, almost too much to ponder in a single listen. In Garcia's "Masterpiece," the tempo is relaxed, and the tone of his vivacious vocals illuminates Dylan's lyrics. The three wicked guitar solos give the listener the time and space needed to relish and absorb the majesty of it all.

Just as the show had begun with a Dylan/Motown one-two wallop, Garcia and his cohorts chase "When I Paint My Masterpiece" with Stevie Wonder's Motown masterpiece, "I Was Made To Love Her." Like "Expressway To Your Heart," Wonder's genius is transformed into a colossal instrumental. The symmetry of this concert is uncanny. *One and one is two. Two and two is four.* On "Expressway," the band latches onto a tight groove before Garcia comes off, but on Wonder's tune, Garcia's *en fuego* from the get-go. Graciously, Jerry defers to Merl, and the funky organ grinder swamps the studio with R&B. Kahn and Kreutzmann crank the tempo, imploring Garcia and Saunders to take it beyond their comfort zone. Like Ali in his prime, Garcia's creative flow is endless. There's never a dull moment, aborted lead, or hesitation of any kind.

Amazingly, this was Garcia's debut of "I Was Made to Love Her," an instrumental he would only perform six times, and never again after 1974. All of this experimentation by Garcia was stunning considering what a groundbreaking year 1972 would be for the Grateful Dead. After a short run of shows at Manhattan's Academy of Music in March, the Dead barnstormed Europe for six weeks, which led to the idiosyncratic triple album, *Europe '72*, which once again showcased the mystical musings of Robert Hunter. On a 100-degree day in August, the Grateful

Dead melted minds with a three-set spectacular on Ken Kesey's farm in Oregon. The band's fall tour was even hotter; but all of this was not enough for Garcia. He was driven to explore and pay homage to the music he cherished. And this band he formed with Saunders and Kahn completed Garcia as an artist. The music would never stop.

The jam on 2-6-72 doesn't need an exclamation point, but Garcia provides the punctuation with Doc Pomus' "Lonely Avenue." Once again, the song symmetry is there—a Stevie Wonder number is followed by a tune that his mentor, Ray Charles, made famous. "Lonely Avenue" also pairs off well with the earlier blues scorcher, "That's All Right." Here's to the slipstreams of imagination that flow through a gifted mind.

During the melancholy intro, Garcia's guitar weeps: "I could cry, I could cry, I could cry...I could die, I could die, I could die. I live on a lonely avenue." Tears fill each syllable as Jerry belts out, "My room has got windows and the sunshine never comes through." And the way he achingly sings, "I live on a Looonleyyyy Ave-ah-nue..." It's pure heartache—the blues minus humor, irony, or defiance. Garcia's voice calls, and his guitar responds patiently to his own pleas.

Garcia lived on the same Lonely Avenue as Doc Pomus and Ray Charles. These musical brothers are bonded by the pain of suffering through unspeakable childhood tragedies. Jerry Felder, who later changed his name to Doc Pomus, was crippled by polio at a young age. Ray Charles Robinson completely lost his eyesight when he was seven, but prior to that, he witnessed the drowning of his brother George in a laundry tub, a vision that would forever haunt him. When Garcia was five, he may have witnessed the drowning death of his father Jose on a fishing trip. It isn't clear whether Jerry actually saw the drowning, or if it became a learned memory from him hearing the story retold; but either way, the pain of losing his father was unbearable. A year earlier, Jerry had two-thirds of the middle finger on his right hand severed as he was steadying wood for his older brother, Tiff. Yes, five-year-old Tiff was swinging the axe that accidentally severed Jerry's finger. Doc, Ray, and Jerry were all too familiar with growing up on Lonely Avenue.

In the heat of this Pacific High "Lonely Avenue," Garcia bends his guitar strings until they screech and scratch with all the surpassed pain of his childhood during the solos, most notably, the second one. The sky's a-crying as Garcia methodically plots his attack and unloads it with the fervor of a preacher prognosticating the apocalypse. Kahn's a demon, thumping with all the madness in his slender frame, prodding Garcia past the point of no return. Climaxing with a mandolin-like tremolo, Garcia kicks on the wah-wah pedal to infuse some final despair. Clearly Garcia is a learned disciple of the blues tradition. This cathartic journey is bound to rattle your bones and shock your brain.

"How Sweet It Is" wraps things up; but after "Lonely Avenue" it's anticlimactic, like watching a battle for bronze. In a rousing ninety-minute romp, Pacific High radiates the talents of Garcia better than any studio release of the Grateful Dead or Jerry Garcia Band. Beyond any shadow of doubt, 2-6-72 features the finest renditions of "Expressway To Your Heart," "That's a Touch I Like," "Save Mother Earth," "I Was Made to Love Her," and "Lonely Avenue." It's a rolling rhapsody of masterpieces in their early prime, raging in all their glory.

In one impromptu performance, Garcia and mates assembled and reinterpreted an anthology of Americana that covered a vast spectrum of musical genres linking legendary lyricists and performers: Dylan, Lennon, Wonder, Charles, Presley, Pomus, Rodgers, Gaye, Saunders, Winchester, Holland-Dozier-Holland, Gamble and Huff. Although Lennon hails from the foreign shores of Liverpool, "Imagine" became an American lullaby, a melody of hope for a burned-out nation. If one were to arrange the originals of these songs for an album, the sum would be the embodiment of essential Americana, perhaps the beginning of a modern companion for Harry Smith's extraordinary *Anthology of American Folk Music* (1952).

Pacific High has gone on to become a consecrated recording for Garcia aficionados, and because it has yet to be officially released, it maintains the alluring appeal of a bootleg. With the plethora of officially released Jerry Garcia Band concerts, I can't fathom why 2-6-72 hasn't met the same fate. Possibly some bootlegs are too hot for public consumption; they're destined to remain in the Bootleg Zone, where only true fanatics can access, trade and obsess over them.

This rambunctious Pacific High jam was a crossroads performance for Garcia who, against his will, had been anointed as the inspirational guru of the Haight-Ashbury scene, just as Dylan had been anointed as the voice of his generation. Dylan's radical break from the folk scene came when he donned a black leather jacket, strapped on an electric guitar, and blasted away the peaceful expectations of those at the 1965 Newport Folk Festival with a performance that was as outrageous as it was courageous. He temporally riled up a few folkies, but more significantly, he turned on and influenced a budding generation of rockers, including the Beatles, The Byrds, Jimi Hendrix, and the Grateful Dead.

Critics and fans have always tried to stamp and label Dylan, but as a solo performer with a lot of nerve, Dylan has remained elusive, dodging other's expectations. On the other hand, Garcia was always trapped by the expectations of his rabid fan base and those in the extended Grateful Dead family who depended on him for their own livelihoods. Garcia could never pull off a Dylan and completely reinvent himself. It's well known that Jerry didn't have a confrontational bone in his body. Captain Trips never desired the leadership role in the Grateful Dead, but sometimes history just crowns its heroes.

As the years rolled by, Garcia would be worshipped by millions. He could never file for divorce from the Grateful Dead, or his hippie kingdom. To cope with this burden, Jerry escaped into a ceaseless assortment of chemical cocktails; but his true love was creating and performing. With Merl Saunders and John Kahn, Garcia formed the nucleus of a band that would sustain him—a shelter from the storm. He found a musical outlet outside of the Grateful Dead without raising any eyebrows or alienating followers. In fact, Deadheads loved and embraced his new band; it was a natural extension of his artistic vision. And this performance in Pacific High Studios was a signpost to the future. The Jerry Garcia Band was busy being born, and it would never fade away.

2

5-28-83 CAPE COD

SAY HELLO TO MY LITTLE FRIEND

"Nothing exceeds like excess" was a popular American myth of the '80s, and no Jerry Garcia Band show embodies that spirit better than this barnburner from the Cape Cod Coliseum. Garcia's audacious performance exhibits key characteristics of two '80s icons who were known by the surname Montana: Joe, the unflappable four-time Super Bowl-winning quarterback of the San Francisco 49ers, and, Tony, the merciless Cuban gangster portrayed by Al Pacino in *Scarface*. Like his San Francisco homeboy, Joe, Garcia orchestrates a stunning and heroic comeback following a lethargic opening set. Just when it sounds like Garcia can't possibly pick any quicker, or extend a solo further, he finds a way to push through previous barriers; redundancy be damned! This kind of overindulgence reminds me of Tony Montana in the final scene of *Scarface*. After snorting a mountain of blow, executing his best friend, and watching his sister, Gina, get gunned down, Montana grabs his M16 rifle and exclaims, "Say hello to my little friend." After all the cussing, snorting, and shooting, Tony turns it up a notch. More is always more, and in the hands of Pacino or Garcia, it's gripping art.

Due to two decades of persistently rampant drug experimentation, Garcia's health had been in serious decline for years. But even seasoned Deadheads were alarmed by his appearance when he took the stage in Cape Cod. Back on 2-6-72, Garcia was the youth of a thousand summers, the hip and happy black-bearded guru of the San Francisco scene. Eleven years later, at the age of forty, Garcia looked like a bedraggled Buddha, a deity visiting from Mt. Olympus. A clever paperback writer could never have conjured up a rock star like Garcia circa 1983: mangy gray hair and matching grungy gray beard, custom-built Tiger guitar planted against a potato-sack physique, squinting eyes peering through gold-rimmed glasses resting on the base of his pale nose, deformed picking hand strumming wildly as the immobile messenger humbly jams in jeans and black T-shirt. And no writer would have ever attached a name as generic as Jerry Garcia to their beastly prodigy.

Yet Garcia's legion of devotees found a sense of certainty in his unworldly presence. When Jerry opened up his soul and sang from the heart, it was like a ray of sunshine bursting through a cloudy day; everybody in the building felt infinitely better. As Jerry stood there and raced through scales, liberated bodies danced and twirled in primal ecstasy. And when Garcia smiled, the collective joy in Jerryville was palpable. No matter how weird things could get inside one's head, there was always the calming, grandfatherly presence of Garcia, offering spiritual rejuvenation through music—no gimmicks.

The Cape Cod drama begins with a rusty rendition of "How Sweet It Is." The six-song first set is flat as a tortilla, but loyal Deadheads yodel and howl anyway—the placebo effect. If there is a tune that moves both the performer and the audience, it's the Hunter/Garcia adaptation of "Gomorrah," from JGB's finest studio effort, *Cats Under the Stars*. Aside from "Gomorrah," the sparks are sparse. Garcia concludes the set with "Run for the Roses," a fine original from his 1982 album with the same name. But it's not a typical set ender showcasing a spectacular "Deal" or "Tangled Up in Blue" jam.

At intermission, this show was a million miles from immortality. If this were the NFL, JGB would be trailing by four touchdowns at the half. To make this a memorable night, Garcia had to blow the roof off the joint in the second set, and he needed a little help from his mates. New to the Jerry Garcia Band on this tour were backing singers Jaclyn LaBranch and Dee Dee Dickerson. These ladies added a potent gospel component to the harmonies. Greg Errico, one of the cofounders of Sly & the Family Stone, had joined JGB on drums six months earlier. It took Jerry a few years to find the ideal replacement for Merl Saunders on organ, but when Melvin Seals joined JGB in 1981, the search ceased. It would be Seals, Kahn, and Garcia until the day Jerry died.

I wonder what was going through Garcia's mind between sets, because when he came out for the second set, he was on a mission. Could he have drawn inspiration from his surroundings? Cape Cod is a cozy New England vacation destination, but the Cape Cod Coliseum, located in South Yarmouth, Massachusetts, was a charmless concrete cube, a haven for World Wide Wrestling Federation events, and a popular touring destination for up and coming heavy metal bands. However, this venue had its place in Grateful Dead history. On October 27, 1979, the Dead thrilled the coliseum with the show of the year, pulling off an astounding Dancing in the Streets > Franklin's Tower combo to start the second set. There had to be some kind of mystical vibe within this faceless dump. In case that wasn't enough, one might suppose, based on Garcia's hyper second set rally with JGB, that there was a pile of pure Peruvian marching powder in Mr. Garcia's dressing room—the type of *yeyo* that would make Tony Montana's eyeball's swim.

Set two of 5-28-83 commences with what sounds like Chuck Berry's "Let it Rock" until Jerry snaps off his jazzy "Rhapsody in Red" lick. It had been four years since this powerhouse, also from *Cats Under The Stars*, had found its way back into the live rotation. The crowd is hyped as Jerry growls, "Let ME hear that...RHAPSODY in Red!" Errico and Kahn hammer away at a wicked pace, clearing a path for Garcia to cut into his first heavy jam of the night—notes crunch and cram in a tidal surge of energy. "Rhapsody in Red" is true-blue Jerry, a fiery fusion of R&B and jazz, a gateway song that sets the night on fire and leads to bolder experimentation down the line.

A fourteen-minute "The Harder They Come" follows the ten-minute opener. With JGB, nothing succeeds like excess. Jerry preaches to his dancing disciples, "As sure as the sun will shine, I'm gonna get my share of what's mine. You know the harder they come, the harder they fall, one and all." The coliseum bounces as one, in sync with Kahn and Errico, and Seals' swampy sound has that righteous Rasta feel. JGB plays it spicy all the way. With each pass, the instrumental interlude becomes more compelling, in spite of the repetitious chord motif. They're invoking an irresistible formula, a time-tested JGB recipe: four rounds of boiling Jerry > two swirling rounds of Melvin's keys > equal parts guitar, drums, bass and keyboard stirred into a chunky groove > a final volley of shooting stars, courtesy of Garcia. The most intriguing section of this Jimmy Cliff cover is the calypso chord shuffle in the middle—Brazilian coffee house music—if there is such a thing. When I hear this groove, I think of percolating java, and I have strange visions of Juan Valdez dancing the fandango. Señor Garcia squeezes a lot of caffeine out of these beans, an anthem that glorifies the struggle of the underdog.

When Garcia was in the thick of a masterful performance with the Grateful Dead, and he felt the time was right to canonize the show, he'd transition into the band's Holy Grail, "Morning Dew." The Cape Cod second set is bound for glory, so Garcia followed "The Harder They Come" with JGB's sacred anthem, "Don't Let Go."

Written by Jesse Stone, "Don't Let Go" soared to the second spot on the R&B charts thanks to a swinging cover by Roy Hamilton in 1958. Commander Cody recorded a rocking "Don't Let Go" in 1974, and five years later, Isaac Hayes served up an arcane disco rendition of the song. Jerry Garcia Band's "Don't Let Go" first appeared in their set list in 1976. The spirit and style of the JGB version resembled Hamilton's hit, except Garcia opted to drop a ten-minute instrumental bomb in the middle. *Say hello to my little friend!*

Inside the coliseum, the crowd is jazzed as Jerry sings, "Hear that whistle at six o'clock (Don't Let Go...Don't Let Go), Come on baby it's time to rock (Don't Let Go...Don't Let Go)." The original lyric is "Hear that whistle at ten o'clock," but if you're performing for gatherings of middle-class hippies, the six o'clock line resonates better. Jaclyn and Dee Dee maintain the "Don't let go, Don't Let go" chant as Jerry howls, "Ahhhhhhh-hold me tight and don't let go-oh," simultaneously picking licks that mimic his growls. That's a touch I like, and it's a tasty prelude to the instrumental bomb.

There's an immediate disconnect from the jovial disposition of the lyrics. Garcia and Kahn forsake civility as they race into uncharted territory. The mood is foreboding, a battered ship being tossed about by an angry sea on a starless night. A rhapsody of darkness emerges—an ideal score for a suspenseful motion picture. Garcia and Kahn are sparring partners exchanging feisty licks as Seals and Errico swirl around them like vultures. Cape Cod is in the grip of four madmen, and the crowd's loving it, cheering them on as if this is the fifteenth round of a championship fight.

JGB was down 28-0 at intermission, but now, Garcia has valiantly led his band to three scores. JGB still trails 28-21, but as sure as the sun will shine, Garcia will lead his mates to the Promised Land, à la Montana. When Joe Cool was smoking along the comeback trail, there was little doubt he'd rally the troops to victory. You could feel the strange magic surge through Candlestick Park. Nobody in American music was better at digging himself out of a hole than Garcia. One of the pitfalls of experimentation is failure, but when a maestro such as Garcia is on a roll, the buzz is undeniable; you feel the sensations rippling through your being. You know the outcome will be rapturous, yet the path that lies ahead is still a mystery.

At some point in just about every JGB set, Jerry played something slowww and easy, a drowsy lullaby, harmless as a mouse, a sort of unannounced intermission during which dancers copped squats, smokers rolled bones, and others migrated towards the hall for a pit stop or a brew. During these dirges, Garcia usually delegated a bass solo for Kahn while he enjoyed a smoke. However, the scenario is different in Cape Cod. Garcia's firing on all cylinders, and hesitation is not an option. Jerry and Melvin slide into a riff that's familiar to almost everyone in Cape Cod. Some are overwhelmed instantly, while others react a few measures later. A dull roar escalates to thunderous adulation as Jerry sings,

"Dear Prudence, won't you come out to play? Dear Prudence, greet the brand new day-ay-ay-ayyyyyyyyy!"

Garcia treasures each line—few things are more rewarding than greeting the brand-new day with the optimism of a child. On the *White Album*, "Dear Prudence" evokes fleeting feelings of joy. At a JGB show, "Dear Prudence" is a religious experience. If any Beatles song conjures up the essence of John Lennon, it's "Dear Prudence." All the illusion in the world won't bring back John, but for as long as Garcia can stretch this out, Lennon's spirit and childlike sanguinity will dance in the hearts of those in JGB Paradise.

With the heinous murder of Lennon on the outskirts of Central Park, and Ronald Regan's ascension to the White House, the dreams and desires of Woodstock Generation were stymied, but not completely snuffed out. The undying spirit of Woodstock resides in a Hendrix solo, a Joplin scream, a Townsend rock opera, a Dylan anthem, and a Sly Stone shout for brotherhood. Between tragic deaths and bands either breaking up or hibernating, there were few surviving Woodstock legends out there bringing people together. Around this time, Dylan was hedging on his commitment to Jesus, and trying to navigate his way through the lost cultural wilderness of the early 1980s. The Grateful Dead and their faithful flock of followers were the last of the Mohicans, still rambling across America, and everywhere they traveled, an impromptu musical celebration came alive. And when the Grateful Dead were resting, JGB was out there keeping hope alive in faceless places like the Cape Cod

Coliseum. As the 5-28-83 "Dear Prudence" materializes, a transcendent moment beckons.

Garcia advances into the "Prudence" improv, squawking and squeaking this way and that way, bending strings with a loving feeling. Flurries of sound swirl—notes and scales cluster into a storm that morphs into a hurricane. The band locks in on Garcia, responsive to his every whim. To anyone who has ever listened to a live "Dear Prudence," it's obvious that Jerry's on his way, and where this glorious aggression will end is anyone's guess. Garcia veers off the trodden path and blasts warning shots, each guitar run slightly sharper and quicker than the one that preceded it. Anticipation builds as the hurricane's eye intensifies.

The defining characteristic of worthy "Prudence" jams are the repetitive riffs that steamroll faster and faster until they fuse into a striking crescendo. In Cape Cod, Garcia's in overdrive as he approaches the summit. His picking velocity challenges sonic reality as the rest of JGB scrambles in pursuit. The fans begin to howl, and the howls turn into a thunderous roar. Garcia receives the energy and redirects it, overwhelming his devotees with a climactic flourish that supersedes anything he's ever done before. It's as if within this aural tornado lay all the secrets on heaven and earth. But ladies and gentlemen, please remember, this is only rock and roll.

Following a "Prudence" crescendo, Garcia usually cuts back to the final verse. But in Cape Cod, Jerry weaves bonus magic, tacking on a two-minute instrumental reprise making this the "Dearest Prudence" of them all. And thanks to the tapers who dodged security and snuck in their recording equipment, this performance lives forever.

There's no rest for the inspired as Garcia rams into "Tangled Up in Blue." Jerry's treatment of Dylan's seven brilliant verses lacks tenderness or conviction. In Cape Cod, the lyrics are like lobster shells; the succulent meat resides in the solos. The first two solos are pressure-packed and lyrical. Launching the final jam, Garcia slings his arrows of desire over and over again. Once upon a time, Jerry was the new sensation, a cherubic-faced prankster with an open heart and a wild mind. In Cape

Cod, Garcia is an obese forty-year-old junkie, but his ashen complexion only adds to his saintly luster when he jams like a God.

Errico challenges Garcia, bashing the skins with all his might. Instinctively, Jerry's a step ahead, racing forward with whatever's left in his enormous tank, and he's tapping into the collective energy reverberating in the concrete cube. Enough is never enough as the epic jam keeps shedding its skin. This is raunchier than a Black Sabbath concert, or one of Vince McMahon's bloody steel cage death matches.

The joint is jumping as JGB leaves the stage. Delirious fans beg for one more bone, and Garcia complies. It's not unusual for JGB to split without an encore, but the faithful coaxed Jerry to pick up his axe and dust off those rusty strings just one more time.

JGB fires up "Midnight Moonlight," a blast from Garcia's bluegrass past as a member of Old & in the Way. This tune, penned by his former bandmate Peter Rowan, was close to Garcia's heart. Everything that's fanciful about bluegrass is now amplified for 7,000 thousand dancing Deadheads. On this enchanted evening, "Midnight Moonlight" dazzles like never before—the vigor of the performance is staggering. Hands down, this is the best vocal performance of the jubilee, and the jam sizzles in the established Jerry > Melvin > Jerry motif. I'm not much of a dancer, but I must kick up an honorary jig every time I hear this "Midnight Moonlight."

Jerry bids farewell to South Yarmouth, Massachusetts, with his lovely lady singers chiming in:

"The ocean is howling for things that might have been. The last good morning sunrise will be the brightest you've ever seen. In the moonlight, in the midnight, in the moonlight midnight moonlight. In the moonlight, in the midnight, in the moonlight midnight moonlight. In the moonlight, in the midnight, in the moonlight midnight moonlight. In the moonlight, in the midnight, in the moonlight midnight moonlight."

Even the fanfare of "Midnight Moonlight" is dramatic. Garcia wasn't the type to bash his guitar à la Pete Townsend, but it would have been a justified reaction to end this raucous affair. This set features Garcia in all his over-indulgent glory, especially the last four songs which are all "best ever" versions. Coming off of such an inauspicious first set, these performances are spectacular theatre—Gonzo JGB! In less than a year's time, the Cape Cod Coliseum was closed down. These days it merely serves as a warehouse for several businesses. For some of us, this South Yarmouth warehouse is hallowed ground, the site of Garcia's greatest blitzkrieg.

3

THE GHOSTS OF SULLIVAN

What constitutes an immortal JGB show? Tell-tale signs of greatness include: waves of creative guitar phrasing, consistently poignant singing, clever song selection that generates relentless momentum, a band that communicates and orchestrates as one as they transform ordinary to extraordinary, and in the process, they create the illusion of stopping time—transcendence. It's rare that all these attributes can coalesce for one group on one night, but that's the way it went down for the Jerry Garcia Band at Music Mountain in South Fallsburg, a forsaken hamlet in Sullivan County, New York.

Once upon a time there was much merriment out in the sticks of Sullivan County. Woodstock, the mother of all music festivals, was held in Bethel, fifteen miles due west of South Fallsburg. This terrain was also the heart of the Catskill Borscht Belt, a string of summer hotels and bungalow colonies that were also known as the Jewish Alps—Disneyland with knishes. From Hendrix, Townsend, Joplin, and Cocker electrifying Hippie Nation on Yasgur's Farm, to Skelton, Streisand, Crosby and Bennett amusing wealthy vacationers at the Concord Hotel, Sullivan County hosted a surplus of ephemeral entertainment magic.

By the '80s, this once-bustling escapist mecca resembled an abandoned honeycomb. Iconic hotels and businesses were now boarded up, and those still standing were passively waiting for the grim reaper. When JGB and their eccentric horde of freaks arrived in South Fallsburg, the area buzzed in a way it hadn't since "Three Days of Peace and Music" back in the summer of '69.

A few days after playing a couple of Keystone gigs, one in Berkeley and one in Palo Alto, JGB arrived at Music Mountain on a rather steamy Wednesday afternoon. Most of the time, a weather report isn't necessary for musical analysis; but for JGB, this was a rare outdoor gig that also featured Bob Weir's band, Bobby & the Midnites. JGB was a nocturnal band accustomed to performing in bars, clubs, dance halls, theatres, gymnasiums and roller-skating rinks—any ol' dark hollow would do. A month earlier, Garcia and Kahn even played an acoustic show at Oregon State Penitentiary in Salem. There wasn't much sunshine or crisp country air on a tour of duty with JGB.

With heavy humidity and the ghosts of Woodstock churning in the Catskill skies, Garcia opens with "How Sweet It Is." The texture and tone of the music embodies the feel of a wondrous outdoor esthetic—a truly bucolic vibe. Garcia's been struck by cupid's arrow. He's smitten with his environment, its arcane historical richness, and the tangible beauty of the here and now—*you know this space is getting hot.* Glancing up at 20,000 or so admirers swaying on the hill, Jerry wants them to feel his love. It also sounds like Garcia is quite comfortable with the band, one of his most cohesive configurations. In addition to the nucleus of Kahn and Seals, Julie Stafford and Liz Stires are now chiming in on vocals. Jimmy Warren's tickling the electric piano, and Billy Kreutzmann is pounding the drums. Kreutzmann joined JGB for a few shows in December of 1981, and he continued touring with them straight through the summer of 1982. Garcia plus Kreutzmann equals phenomenal chemistry.

Unlike the Cape Cod show, where the leader of the band was sluggish out of the gate, Garcia's leads sparkle at the start of "How Sweet It

Is." During a succinct keyboard interlude, Saunders and Warren splish and splash back and forth in rhyme. Jimmy Warren is the all-time mystery man of JGB. He didn't have much of a musical resume before joining the band, and he didn't fluff up his resume much after his departure. The consensus amongst Dead critics is that he wasn't much of a player. For the duration of his stint, which covered most of 1981 and 1982, Warren's keyboards were low in the mix. On tapes of other shows from the Warren era, I have to really focus to detect his presence; but his contributions are audible and appealing on the Music Mountain tape. There's nothing worse than a mediocre musician who sticks out like a sore thumb in a group setting, like, say, Vince Welnick did with the Grateful Dead in the '90s. Warren may not have been a piano prodigy, but at least his efforts meshed with the direction of the music.

In a beguiling exhibition, Garcia drives the last "How Sweet It Is" solo around the block three times. The singing returns and the harmonies are splendid. JGB employed many fine female singers over the years, including the dynamic combo of Donna Jean Godchaux and Maria Muldaur in 1978, but Stafford and Stires have the complementary touch. They strike the right frequency, shining light on the golden tones of the gray-bearded guru, who delivers the chorus in a euphoric outburst:

"How sweet it is to be loved by you...Sweeter than the honey from the bees, baby! How sweet it is to be loved by you...Yes it is, you know it is, bay-beee!"

Crooning with the angels at Music Mountain, Garcia is in peak form, deftly mixing passion with perfect pitch all night long. Most prodigious vocalists hone their talents at a younger age, but Garcia didn't really come into his own as a vocalist until the *Workingman's Dead/American Beauty* era. For the Grateful Dead's first four years, most observers felt Pig Pen, with his alpha male blues voice, was the group's premier singer. But once "Ripple," "Casey Jones," and "Friend of the Devil" were heard on the airwaves, it became crystal-clear that Garcia was blossoming into a superb vocalist with a distinctive style. By 1982, his voice was operating on higher ground. Garcia remained a master vocalist until the day he died, but his vocal chords, which were worn down by years of excessive smoking, didn't always cooperate. Music Mountain is a watershed performance. It may be the last time Garcia's diaphragm, abdomen, lungs, trachea, thorax, and nasal passages worked in conjunction to flawlessly express the sounds swirling in his soul.

Garcia usually needed a few warm-up tunes to take his guitar playing to an inspired state. Once inside his sphere of excellence, Garcia could take a frequently played song and mold it into a masterpiece that would blow away anything that had transpired before. And due to its immense nature, it could never be played that way again. At Music Mountain, Garcia had the Right Stuff from the moment he took the stage, and the second song of the night, "Catfish John," was absolutely miraculous.

Written by Bob McDill and Allen Reynolds, "Catfish John" was a minor 1972 country hit for Johnny Russell, who's best known for co-writing "Act Naturally," which was popularized by Buck Owens, and then the Beatles. Russell's most famous hit, "Rednecks, White Socks and Blue Ribbon Beer," peaked at the fourth spot on the Billboard country charts in 1973. That same year, Russell performed "Catfish John" on *The Wilburn Brothers Show,* a syndicated TV program showcasing popular hillbilly troubadours. With his well-cropped mustache and beard, Russell's mug screamed Okie from Muskogee; but standing there, guitar in hand, "Big" Johnny was plump as a pumpkin in his orange suit, which looked as if it were standard issue from the Tennessee State Penitentiary. Russell's focused, stoic stage presence bore an uncanny resemblance to Garcia in the '80s.

Garcia first strummed "Catfish John" on banjo with Old & in the Way in '73, and in a few years, it would become another dandy in JGB's bag of tricks. In preparation for his South Fallsburg fishing trip, Garcia tunes up his strings and engages his MU-TRON envelope filter. Perhaps there has never been a guitar effect more closely associated to a guitar player than the MU-TRON envelope filter is to Garcia. The effect produces a nasally quack that is an essential part of Grateful Dead favorites like "Shakedown Street," "Feel Like a Stranger," "Fire on the Mountain," and "Estimated Prophet." The effect is especially enticing as Garcia strikes the first mighty "Catfish" chord—*WHAP*—a massive fish beckons.

"Bonp, bomp-bomp-bomp...A-whomp-bomp-bomp...Bonp, bomp-bomp-bomp...A-whomp-bomp-bomp." The beat squirts forward—a content catfish trudges through a black, muddy river. Garcia and his gals harmonize:

"Mama said, 'Don't go near that river. Don't be hanging around, old Catfish John. Come the morning I'll always be there, walking in his footsteps in the sweet Delta dawn.'"

The imagery is evocative as Jerry transports us *to a town so long ago, where the sweet magnolias blossom,* and *cotton fields were white as snow.* Yes, this is the lonesome plight of a slave turned river hobo, but Garcia's spirited vocal rejoices in the beauty of nature, and in the virtues of friendship. In spite of maternal warnings, the narrator is drawn to Catfish John, and reputation be damned, he's proud to be Catfish John's friend. It's the kind of outsider/outlaw ballad that the Grateful Dead championed; songs such as "Wharf Rat," "Me and My Uncle," "Stagger Lee," "Big River," "Brown Eyed Women," and "Mexicali Blues." But none of those songs ever roared like the mighty "Catfish" of Music Mountain.

As the sun fades west, a sublime jam materializes out of the sticky South Fallsburg night. Garcia and Kahn zip through scales in a comic strip of sound; it's as if the music's playing the band. As one door closes, another opens—like a secret underwater language amongst whales. Garcia hands off to Warren, who then passes the baton to Seals. JGB's in the midst of their reggae shuffle, and the timing is immaculate, with articulate punctuation on each passage. Garcia seizes the spotlight again. His leads accelerate and mutate into a psychedelic cyclone leading to the "Catfish" climax. Garcia crosses the anticipated finish line with so much momentum that he has to improvise a post crescendo extension.

His axe yields lightning strikes, from the earth to the heavens. It's a "Catfish" supreme, another notch on Garcia's belt of immortality.

Half of the crowd is cheering, the other half is silently stupefied by what they've just seen. Another shrill guitar blast celebrates the arrival of Little Milton's blues stomp, "That's What Love Will Make You Do," recorded in Memphis, at Stax Records. During the first three numbers, Garcia has steered the music from Detroit to Nashville to Memphis in a most peculiar, yet linear way. In the musical hierarchy of his mind, Garcia builds the bridges that logically link these songs. "How Sweet It Is," "Catfish John" and "That's What Love Will Make You Do," was a frequently played JGB triple shot; but these Music Mountain performances are shining stars that never age or lose their luster.

We've reached that part of the show were Garcia usually drags on a slow joint like "Russian Lullaby" or Dylan's "Simple Twist of Fate." Fortuitously, on 6-16-82, Garcia opts for "Valerie," one of Hunter's contributions on *Run for the Roses,* the latest and greatest Garcia recording debacle. The studio "Valerie" is a spineless bimbo. In her natural live environment at Music Mountain, "Valerie" is the belle of the ball. Garcia pleads:

"Hey now, baby, What did I do? I shot my dog 'cause he growled at you. Hey, Valerie, won't you be good to me?"

It's blues to the core, but Garcia operates on a different frequency than other musicians. The "Valerie" solo is volatile and succinct (by JGB standards), although it's twice the duration of a prototype blues solo. This is all Jerry; no organ grinding or funky chord play. It's a pattern-breaker, a lucid path in a maze of expeditions.

JGB would never play "Valerie" or "Catfish John" again after 1986. My guess is that Garcia never took the time to relearn either one following his recovery from the diabetic coma that knocked him out of commission for a few months in '86. Jerry survived his brush with death, but the coma claimed some of his repertoire. It's a shame because "Valerie" is a vastly underappreciated tune, and as of the publishing date of this book, no live JGB version has ever been released.

Garcia was a bluegrass aficionado with an equally keen palate for the blues, soul, and jazz, and he had a predilection for Dylan tunes. But perhaps, most of all, Jerry loved those first generation rock and rollers, and nothing exemplifies that better than the fifth song in the Music Mountain lineup, Chuck Berry's "Let it Rock." JGB bursts into an instantly pulsating chord progression with a soulful bounce, the type of hook that you can groove to for hours. Some nights there's inexplicable mojo in the strangest of places if you listen to it right. Freaks are buzzing and bouncing mountainside as Garcia sings:

"She don't love me hear them singing in the sun. Payday's coming and my work is all done."

An urgent sonic escalation ensues. Garcia's possessed solo is a steel-driving tribute to the working man. Kreutzmann and Kahn clear the way like offensive tackles as Garcia hits the gaps. The potential of what can happen within structured improvisation is fully realized—textbook rock and roll, thunderous and proud. Garcia continues to let it rock with a sizzling "Deal" to conclude a most impressive opening set.

Money, who needs it. I live a life free and easy. A toothbrush in my hand. Let me be a traveling man. I'm a roadrunner, babe.

Set two is under way with "(I'm a) Road Runner," a 1966 hit for Junior Walker & the All Stars, penned by the songwriting trio of Holland-Dozier-Holland. The opening song of the show, "How Sweet It Is," was also penned by that legendary trio. Once again there's that natural balance to Garcia's song selections, a skill that gives his best performances the feel and purpose of a well-conceived album. Garcia is still picking a wicked guitar early on side two of 6-16-82 Music Mountain. In "Road Runner," Garcia found a song that expresses his mindset as a rambling troubadour, and it also expresses the collective carefree philosophy of his audience. "Road Runner" is the Deadhead milieu in a nutshell—the restless soul on the road yearning for a dream that's just out of reach, but ultimately, the pursuit is where the fun is.

As darkness touches down on Music Mountain, the band slips into a sophisticated "Love in the Afternoon," highlighted by Garcia's gorgeous singing. There's really no reference point to describe Garcia's vocal style. Sinatra, Dylan, Redding, Jagger, Cash, Plant, McCartney; all have distinctive voices, with reference points and vocal influences you can trace. I draw a blank when I try to compare Garcia to another singer, that's how distinctive his sound is. The voice exists in its own realm, Tupelo Honey tapped straight from his heart.

The post-serenade "Love in the Afternoon" jam moseys into an exotic tropical landscape. You're on a beach in Jamaica after a mind-altering experience and the sun is rising like a runny yolk as your skin melts into the sand. It's a moody exploration painted with psychedelic splashes, and with it, the tension of the show slowly dissipates. Sir Isaac Newton's law of gravity takes hold. What comes up, must come down.

JGB dives into "Don't Let Go," and it comes off like a love letter to the Music Mountain faithful.

I'm so happy to have you here
(Don't let go, don't let go)
Keeps me grinnin' from ear to ear
(Don't let go, don't let go)
Ooh wee
This feeling's killing me
Oh, shucks
I wouldn't stop for a million bucks
I love you so
Just hold me tight and don't let go
(Don't let go, don't let go)
Hold me tight and don't let go
(Don't let go, don't let go)

In comparison to the gonzo Cape Cod version, this "Don't Let Go" eases down the road as if the band were jamming at a jazz festival.

Garcia rolls like Sonny Rollins until he splits for a mid-song smoke during a curt Kreutzmann drum solo. Kahn checks into the percussions with some tantalizing bass runs, and then Garcia stubs his smoke and rejoins the conversation. It's not a top shelf "Don't Let Go," but the jazz cats give it a helluva ride. The bubble's burst, and only a pair of jingles remain.

With a hellacious rainstorm on the horizon, and Bobby & the Midnites waiting in the wings, JGB had to simmer down. For this mini-tour, Bobby and Jerry alternate who opens, and Jerry won the lottery, for this is the night to play first. However, the crowd is still pumped beyond belief as Garcia's golden pipes lay down a stunning, "The Night They Drove Old Dixie Down." Rolling yodels and "Yee-haws" accompany every line.

JGB's "The Night They Drove Old Dixie Down" is a compelling dirge that conjures up raw emotion on par with any Civil War reenactment or documentary. Garcia croons a timeless eulogy which mourns the coldest and bloodiest years of America's existence, or, on this night on Music Mountain, the sadness conveys the loss of music legends like Pig Pen, Janis and Jimi, or it could even be a eulogy for the Catskills. A great sense of loss is conveyed, and all that remains are the healing powers of music.

> *The night they drove old Dixie down*
> *All the people were singing*
> *They went, "Na la, na, na, na, na...la, na, na, , na, na, na, nah..."*

Off to the races, JGB finishes the show with an anti-climactic "Run for the Roses." Garcia might have had big ideas, but the cash was all spent. In a different circumstance, Garcia may have followed "Dixie" with "Dear Prudence" or "Tangled Up in Blue," but the clock was ticking, and Garcia had to abdicate his throne.

As the torrential rains twisted Music Mountain into a muddy quagmire, Garcia was reminiscing at the nearby Concord Hotel with Grateful

Dead road manager Rock Scully. According to Scully's book, *Living With the Dead*, Garcia walked into the 3,000-seat dining room, and said, "Take a good look at this dining room, Rock. Bill Graham actually waited these tables! Mickey Hart's grandparents, the Tessels, came here every summer and *Bill Graham* used to WAIT ON THEM!"

Cosmic Charlie, how do you do? The Concord had seen better days, but who has not? The colossal Catskills resort would shut its doors for good in 1998. Nothing seems to stick in the sticks of Sullivan. The fabled hotels have been left for ruin, or they've been demolished by the merciless wrath of a wrecking ball. Even mighty Music Mountain, which hosted summer concerts for only two years, was closed for business by the end of 1982. Currently, condos stand in the sacred fields where JGB once soared on a summer's night. But we'll always have the crystal-clear audience recordings captured on that mountainside—Prozac for future generations. Viva Music Mountain!

Hold me tight and don't let go. Garcia and Kahn at
Music Mountain, 6-16-82. ©Bob Minkin

4

MIRACLE BY THE LAKE

February 1980 was a memorable month for both the Jerry Garcia Band and the US Olympic hockey team. The night before Garcia played Laker Hall on the SUNY Oswego campus, the upstart American hockey team thrashed Czechoslovakia 7-3 in Lake Placid, New York, 181 miles northeast of Oswego. Czechoslovakia, a former Soviet satellite, was favored to win the silver medal in ice hockey. It was a foregone conclusion that the Soviet Union would stomp on and bludgeon any team that stood between them and a sack full of Olympic gold. After the baby-faced Americans smoked Czechoslovakia, the impossible dream was hatched. Just maybe, on their home ice, if everything in the universe lined up perfectly, these fearless American kids could give the Russians a fight, and if it's a fight, the outcome can't be certain. Peculiar things were happening in upstate New York.

If any American icon was comfortable with the concept of an uncertain outcome, it was Garcia. His entire career as a performing artist was an outrageous crap shoot, a psychedelic explosion into an unparalleled realm of weirdness. To quote Hunter S. Thompson: "When the going gets weird, the weird turn pro." Garcia was the consummate pro, combining the yin and yang of improbability with steadfast dedication to his craft. Out of the thin air off the shores of Lake Ontario, and in the shadows of Oswego's Nine Mile Point Nuclear Station, Garcia pumped out the penultimate version of JGB's extravagant After Midnight > Eleanor Rigby > After Midnight trilogy. For those who bought the ticket and took the ride in Laker Hall, it was a long, strange and giddy trip indeed.

Along with Kahn on bass, this bare-bones JGB quartet included Ozzie Ahlers on keyboards and Johnny de Foncesca on drums. Garcia was still shuffling band members in search of a certain sound. In 1979, Garcia, Saunders, and Kahn toured as Reconstruction, with a trombone and sax player, but this project lacked the X factor of previous lineups. Reconstruction was Saunders' last tour with Garcia. In the autumn of 1979, Garcia started playing gigs and practicing with a new quartet— Jerry Garcia Band was born again. By the time JGB played their first 1980 East Coast gig at Lisner Auditorium in Washington, DC on February 12, they were kicking ass and taking names. Garcia had the Right Stuff—a rotation of songs that displayed his eclectic tastes and ignited his guitar wizardry. There was more Garcia in the band than ever before, and Jerry was physically and mentally ready for the challenge. Robert Hunter joined the tour in Oswego, and opened for JGB. The beloved bard's acoustic set was a howling dash through Grateful Dead anthems, and some lesser-known originals, accented by choppy, chaotic strumming—Dylanesque in temperament.

Promontory Riders: Robert Hunter and JGB at Kean
College, 2-28-80 ©Jay Blakesberg

JGB's performance commences with "I'll Take a Melody," an Allen Toussaint composition that appears on Garcia's third solo album, *Reflections* (1976). Toussaint performs "I'll Take a Melody" with a lively Cajun bounce, while Garcia's interpretation is deliberate and deeply spiritual. Music was Garcia's religion, and "I'll Take a Melody" was one of his favorite psalms. Garcia brings out the essence of so many songs, but this time, "I'll Take a Melody" brings out the essence of Garcia:

You know I've been called a dreamer
Dreams that never come true
But I've been called so many things before
Tell you what I'm gonna do

I'll take a melody
And see what I can do about it

I'll take a simple C to G
And feel brand new about it

Few could illuminate the limitless potential of a simple chord progression like Garcia. For a long time, I was under the impression that
"I'll Take a Melody" was a Hunter/Garcia composition. It has a personal
touch, as if Hunter penned it for Garcia, just as he had done on another
Reflections track, "Mission in the Rain." "Melody" is a wonderful set
opener, but Garcia sounds like he has rice cakes lodged in his esopha-
gus. His voice is unusually ragged in Laker Hall; however, there's nothing ragged in his fluid and expressive guitar phrasing.

"Friend of the Devil" is a promising selection in the second spot,
but the performance is a complete bust—an adored anthem is dragged
through the mud. In addition to Jerry's scruffy voice, it sounds as though
he's nodding out on stage. After a sloppy guitar solo, Garcia returns to a
verse instead of singing the "Got two reasons why I cry" bridge.

After the hideous "Devil," Garcia pushes the reset button, opting
to play his favorite opening combo, "How Sweet It Is" and "Catfish
John." It's a prudent decision. JGB turns in solid performances as the
knots in Jerry's vocal chords begin to untie. The circulating audience
recording from Laker Hall is good with two exceptions: there's a nasty
cut as the band peaks on the "Catfish John" jam, and one imbecile yells
"Sit down!" at least a dozen times during, "How Sweet it is." As old and
bitter as I may one day become, I'll never become so belligerent that
I'll yell at, or even politely ask, someone to sit down at a rock and roll
show. Quality live music is more of an aural experience than a visual
one, and it's more emotional than analytical. If you're the type of person
that pesters someone for expressing themselves by dancing, you need to
stop wasting your money on concerts. Try a museum, shopping arcade,
casino, or bingo parlor.

Talking about gambling, Garcia shuffles the deck, and on the fifth
song of the night, he draws an ace with a Grateful Dead favorite, "Deal."
JGB first performed "Deal" at the Keystone Berkeley on 10-7-79, the

debut gig of the current quartet. It was an enhanced version with, you guessed it, more jam. Garcia's new "Deal" would electrify Oswego, and alter the trajectory of the show.

Vocal struggles lesson as Garcia rolls through the opening verses. The sharp twangs from the strings of his mighty guitar jolts everybody out of their seats, even the guy who was yelling "Sit down!" Ozzie Ahlers cut in with a synthesized solo that retraces Garcia's footsteps. Jerry responds with a few more fiery rounds. Garcia's followers rejoice in the new "Deal," and they sing the final line with Garcia, louder and bolder:

Don't you let that Deal go down
Don't you let that DEAL go down
Don't you let that DEAL GO DOWN
DON'T YOU LET THAT DEAL GO DOWN!!!"

A tight, chord-driven jam follows, a jam that's more significant than it is impressive. This is the beginning of the showcase "Deal" solo that would end so many sets for both Garcia Band and the Grateful Dead in the '80s. The appeal of this "Deal" is the shared excitement between the band and the audience as a beloved song is transcending into a vehicle with infinite possibilities.

Following a pair of Grateful Dead originals and three trademark JGB covers, a wise analyst might prognosticate that a Dylan song is blowing in the wind. The crowd erupts when Jerry sings, "You got a lot of nerve to say you are my friend. When I was down you just stood there grinning." Garcia's "Positively 4th Street" is the polar opposite of Dylan's snarly version, which compresses angry lyrics against a jovial musical landscape. With "Positively 4th Street," which has been characterized as a finger-pointing song, Dylan once again raised the bar of artistic imagination. Garcia first performed "Positively 4th Street" in 1973 on *Live at Keystone* with Merl Saunders. In an interview with David Gans, Garcia said,

"It was the beautiful sound of 'Positively 4th Street' that got to me more than the bitterness of the lyric. The combination of the beauty and the bitterness, to me, is wonderful. It's like a combination of something being funny and horrible—it's a great combination of two odd ingredients in the human experience."

Jerry's trembling voice serves his heart up on a platter. The visceral feelings that moved Dylan to pen "Positively 4th Street" are fully and honestly explored by Garcia's mournful wails. The piercing blues solos scream in agony. They're reminiscent of Miles Davis' sound on *Sketches of Spain*. Jerry's "4th Street" rolls on for twelve minutes, and there's not an ounce of fat to slice off. This song is quite an emotional undertaking, and that's probably why Garcia rarely played it. With a major performance in the rearview mirror, the set ends with a bodacious "That's All Right Mama." The cosmic shift of energy within this show after the lame start is something to behold.

When like minds reconvene for set two, it's as if set one never ended. Kahn's trampoline bass beats triggers "Money Honey," and Garcia's spraying the pepper. Another JGB classic penned by Jesse Stone, "Money Honey" was a number one hit for Clyde McPhatter and the Drifters in 1953, and it was also covered by Eddie Cochran and Elvis. In Oswego, Garcia's bewildering the kids on campus by racing through just about every guitar scale known to man. Without the soulful presence of Saunders or Seals, or background singers for that matter, Garcia's thrust into the role of rock and roll hero. Always the focal point of JGB, Garcia's guitar playing is more dominant than ever in this quartet—his every musical whim is clearly amplified.

Garcia was a maestro with refined tastes. Certain songwriters stirred his muse, and Jimmy Cliff was one of those guys. JGB fills the second spot of set two with "Sitting In Limbo." After a relaxed and reflective instrumental, Garcia pours his budding emotions into the song's bridge:

I don't know what life will show me
But I know what I've seen

I can't say where life will lead me
But I know where I've been
Try my hand at love and friendship
But all that is past and gone
This little boy is moving on

The beautiful passage is greeted with noisy approval from those in attendance on this fateful Sunday. Laker Hall is the sanctuary, and Jerry's preaching a peaceful sermon. Like "I'll Take a Melody," "Sittin' in Limbo" suits Garcia's style and it shares his sentiments. JGB revs the engine back up for "Let it Rock." Neil Young's mantra of the day was *Hey hey, my my, rock and roll will never die*, and on this night it's the JGB battle cry. Garcia's guitar sprints are livid—it sounds like somebody gave him a hotfoot prior to the second solo. Garcia chooses an aggressive course on just about every solo. Maybe he was tapping into the abundance of energy produced by the turbulent weather, which dumps ten to twenty feet of lake-effect snow on Oswego every winter. If you take the opening solo from the Music Mountain "Let it Rock," and pair it with the second solo from 2-17-80, you'd have created a rather ferocious beast.

After a groggy start, Garcia hits the reset button, and starting with that springboard "Deal," every ensuing performance is sublime. The twists, turns and peaks of this unruly show coalesce into JGB's definitive masterpiece, After Midnight > Eleanor Rigby > After Midnight.

The crowd has no idea what's in store as they enthusiastically greet "After Midnight." The "Eleanor Rigby" interlude is a flash of inspiration that was born on 1-20-80 at the Keystone Palo Alto. On that occasion, it was more of a suggestive tease than a jam. As the tour progressed, "Eleanor Rigby" blossomed into a well-defined three-minute jam. On 2-12-80, JGB blitzed Washington, DC with a stunning performance of this trio. Oswego is about to get their fair share.

Gliding into "After Midnight," JGB establishes a pleasing groove that initially seeks to eliminate the constraints of time. There's a driving pulse to JJ Cale's iconic anthem that demands resolution in a reasonable amount of time. In 1970, Eric Clapton helped canonize "After Midnight" with a tight, impassioned studio track that became an instant FM classic. Garcia continues to strip the hustle out of "After Midnight" by singing the lyrics in a soft, thoughtful manner. Garcia identifies massive potential in the jam, but he must first break down the song's foundation in order to roam free.

Still buzzing from "Let it Rock," Garcia unloads on "After Midnight," and Ozzie adds a colorful keyboard run. Ahlers' contributions in JGB are underappreciated. Enthusiasts who have spent years listening to bootleg tapes featuring either Saunders or Seals as the keyboardist have become accustomed to a thick, rich, funky groove. Ahlers' style didn't complement the overall sound as well, but his solos were aggressive. I like the way Ozzie played cat and mouse with Garcia. Ahlers listened closely to Jerry, and he answered the Bearded One often by mimicking his phrasing in the classic blues call and response motif. In response to Ahlers' synthesized solos, Garcia raised the intensity level of his playing. This quartet pushed Garcia out of his comfort zone, and for the most part, the results are fabulous.

Garcia intently moves towards "Eleanor Rigby," guns a-blazing. Kahn, Ahlers, and de Foncesca forge ahead—funky and self-assured. Garcia plays over a beat that sounds something like the Phil Rizzuto part of "Paradise by the Dashboard Light." Garcia rides the waves, weaving in and out and all round. Bass blasts rattle the walls as Johnny's drumming fills the halls. Young Johnny is realizing his dream, playing drums in the big leagues for the first time. Later in the year, an automobile crash would claim his life. Johnny's premature passing is tragic, but his beat lives on in the hearts and minds of JGB fans.

There's a mischievous temperament to the instrumental—the musicians are in the thick of something divine, sucked into a creative vortex. They're a band of pirates hijacking the collective imagination of the crowd. Garcia and mates are fully engaged in "After Midnight," yet their sensing of the impending "Eleanor Rigby" creates a dynamic effect. This exotic combination allows JGB the opportunity to go places where only the Grateful Dead roam. During combos like Scarlet Begonias > Fire on the Mountain, Estimated Prophet > Eyes of the World and Not Fade Away > Going Down the Road Feeling Bad > Not Fade Away, the Grateful Dead embellished and extended the segues and transitions, turning them into an idiosyncratic art form. As they would move into a new song, they often found themselves still partially planted in the old one. They played in the past, present, and future simultaneously. In Laker Hall, Garcia is in transition paradise. His playing is remarkable as he approaches "Eleanor Rigby," or, as the case may be, as he says so long to "After Midnight." Let's just call this an "After Midby" jam.

Hysteria grips Oswego as JGB enters the haunting Beatles melody. Garcia's guitar weeps a universal anthem that expresses the eternal sadness and compassion of humanity. "Eleanor Rigby" swoops in out of nowhere—a cosmic zap to the medulla of the unsuspecting audience. After two delicate rounds of "Rigby," JGB accelerates the pace to double time. The twisted psychedelic dream is now a polished jazz moment—Kahn and Garcia are fulfilling their purpose, wreaking havoc as only they can. Before easing back into "After Midnight," Garcia bids farewell to "Rigby" and welcomes "Midnight" with careening chord progressions that test the elasticity of Eastern and Western music theory. It's a shooting star, another segue masterpiece that balances the brilliance of the "After Midby" jam. Let's call this the "Eleanor Rignight" jam.

After reprising "After Midnight" with a few lightly sung verses, Garcia and mates charge in classic rock attack mode. Garcia shows off his predilection for repetitious licks that vary slightly in velocity with each new sequence. This Oswego reprise is thrilling, but it's not as dramatic as the one from Kean College eleven nights later. However, the 2-17-80 After Midnight > Eleanor Rigby > After Midnight, as a whole, reigns supreme. It's one of Señor Garcia's great conquests. This mighty trio would be played for the final time at The Stone in San Francisco on

3-8-80. This definitive JGB masterpiece trifecta arrived out of nowhere, and disappeared just as easily.

Garcia Band could have split Oswego as conquering kings, but they tacked two more tunes on to an already epic show. The first one, Dylan's "It Takes a Lot to Laugh, It Takes a Train to Cry," is sluggish compared to other versions, but that's the way Jerry opts to play it on this tour. It took me a few listens to appreciate Garcia's nifty fret work on this understated Oswego version.

"The Harder They Come" is a symmetrical closer for this eclectic gig. Garcia performed two songs each from Jimmy Cliff, Bob Dylan, Elvis Presley, and the Grateful Dead. No matter how weird things seem, there were always guiding principles and themes pulling Garcia's performances together—chaos and order thriving side by side, even if Garcia didn't consciously plan it that way.

Without the soulful persuasions of Seals or Saunders, "The Harder They Come" had a Russian vibe that could've inspired a massive folk dance in Red Square. The instrumental set off unabashed revelry in Laker Hall. There's something joyfully defiant in the texture of the music, as if it's foreshadowing a David beats Goliath moment. *As sure as the sun will shine, I'm gonna get my share of what's mine.*

Herb Brooks had his team of college kids and amateurs on lockdown, eating, dreaming, and breathing hockey immortality. But who's to say that some of those dreamers might not have snuck out of the Olympic Village for an inspirational field trip to Oswego? Jim Craig (goalie) looked like a Deadhead. If you can indulge this fantasy, then these hungry kids would have experienced the American Dream in a rock and roll band—a pair of rookies and two veterans keeping hope alive, creating transcendence in a time when it was needed most. Between the hostage crisis in Iran and the Soviet occupation in Afghanistan, Americans waiting in endless gas lines longed for something to celebrate. In a rapacious two-hour show in Laker Hall, JGB fueled the "Miracle by the Lake." Five days later, there was that "Miracle on Ice." David beat Goliath 4-3. Those were the days. It almost makes me sentimental for the Cold War.

5

LEGION OF MARY'S
RESTLESS FAREWELL

There were those who thought Bob Dylan's best songwriting days were behind him after his 1966 motorcycle mishap on Ohayo Mountain Road near his Woodstock home. In the seven years that followed the accident heard round the world, Dylan's songwriting style simplified, and his musical output diminished. When Dylan unveiled *Blood on the Tracks* the critical praise gushed fast and furious. The voice of his generation was now a maturing artist sharing his life wisdom, and writing lyrics that dared to say things about love and relationships that have never been heard before in song. Dylanheads were rightfully overjoyed; but lost in the haze of effusive *Blood on the Tracks* praise was Dylan's first album of 1974, *Planet Waves*. It's one of my favorite albums, and it has to be one of Garcia's as well. Jerry went on to cover three songs from *Planet Waves*: "Going, Going, Gone," "Forever Young," and "Tough Mama." In San Francisco's Great American Music Hall, on the 199th birthday of the United States of America, Garcia performed a "Tough Mama" that may be his finest Dylan cover, ever.

Garcia, Saunders, and Kahn's current band began to take shape in July of '74, when they added Martin Fierro (sax and flute) and Paul Humphrey (drums) to the lineup. At the end of that year, Ron Tutt replaced Humphrey on drums, and the band took on the moniker Legion of Mary. Two days after this Great American Music Hall show, Legion of Mary would play for the final time at the Keystone Berkeley. On 7-4-75, they are peaking as a band, comfortable as ever in their collective skin. The Legionnaires sound self-assured and loose as they launch "Tough Mama" to open set two. In particular, every sax note is perfectly pitched and placed, which wasn't always the case. Garcia is smitten with "Tough Mama,"—his admiration is blatant as he croons:

Tough mama, meat shaking on your bones.
I'm going, going down to the river and get you a stone
Papa's on the highway, that steel driving crew
Sister's in the big house, her working days are through
Tough mama, can I blow a little smoke on you?

If somebody wrote "Tough Mama" today, that individual would be hailed as "The Poet Laureate of the New Millennium." But few write or perform songs like this anymore. On *Planet Waves* Dylan sings "Tough Mama" with all the sexual swagger he could muster, and The Band backs Dylan with a bronco-busting arrangement. Garcia picks up on that Wild, Wild West vibe as he takes "Tough Mama" for a ride. Blazing through the opening passage, Garcia's axe whips up a dust storm. Ron Tutt, who formerly toured with Elvis, lays down intricate drum fills, ensuring happy trails for Garcia. The synchronicity of the band is stunning. At times Legion of Mary was longwinded, and Fierro's sax shrieked too much, but the second and third instrumentals, featuring Saunders and Fierro respectively, flow with the certainty of an ancient river. Before delivering the knockout blow, Garcia sings:

A day in the countryside was hotter than a crotch
I stood alone upon a ridge and all I did was watch
Tough mama, must be time to carve another notch

Dylan's lyric is "Sweet goddess must be time to carve another notch." Lyrical accuracy be damned, because Garcia's passions are perverse as he rides "Tough Mama" again. Provocative guitar phrasing is accented by sharp tones and rapid-fire licks. It's a stunning solo from the start, and the momentum just spirals from there. After three euphoric melody loops, Garcia had executed a masterful solo, but inexplicably, he adds another round, and in doing so, he challenges himself to play something more climactic than before. And as he pulls off the impossible crescendo, the normally chill Frisco crowd goes berserk. The roar's clearly audible on the soundboard recording. For a moment, the Great American Music Hall explodes like Madison Square Garden.

Enthusiasm surges through the final verse. Garcia's voice tingles, "I ain't hauling any of my lambs to the marketplace anymore," and it's followed by a tasty guitar flourish—"beedle-bee, beedle-bee, beedle-boo." Garcia: "Prison wall are tumbling down, there ain't no end in sight. I gained some recognition but I lost my appetite. Tough Mama, meet me at the border late tonight." Garcia fires away; the promise of another solo is in the air, as crazy as it may seem, and then it's suddenly aborted. The band pulls the plug with jaw-dropping precision.

A decade after Garcia's death, Rhino Records released *Legion of Mary*, a double CD of performances from various shows. It's a pleasing collection that reflects favorably upon the Legion of Mary stint. The 7-4-75 "Tough Mama" is the opening track of this compilation. Bravo! Job well done, Rhino. If you enjoy the music of Garcia, this is mandatory listening.

Legion of Mary's set lists didn't gel as rationally and smoothly as they did in other Garcia configurations. "Little Sunflower" follows

"Tough Mama." That's like serving shrimp cocktail with apple sauce. "Little Sunflower" is a lovely jazz composition penned by the esteemed trumpeter Freddie Hubbard. Garcia whittles away early on, establishing a Wes Montgomery-like groove as Kahn counters with coy bass runs. It's an easy listen with a Sunday brunch at the bistro feel, but there's a complete disconnect from the intensity of "Tough Mama." As "Little Sunflower" attempts to blossom, Saunders digs up soil and plants seeds. By the time Fierro jumps in, "Little Sunflower" becomes a more effective sleep aid than Ambien. Legion of Mary had a knack for playing an instrumental or two like this every night, but these selections did little to propel momentum. Looking back on "Little Sunflower," I enjoy the ambiance of the music and appreciate the gesture.

The following rocker, Hank Ballard's "Tore Up Over You," would have been a logical choice on the heels of "Tough Mama." Garcia never drifted too far from those rhythm and blues tunes that filled up his adolescent years. Young Jerome must have had a helluva 78 collection. Garcia recorded "Tore Up Over You" for *Reflections*, a deftly arranged batch of originals and covers that reveals Jerry's musical soul. "Tore Up Over You" was ridiculously hot during JGB's 1980 tour. This Great American Music Hall rendition ripples and wiggles with a boogie-woogie feeling.

"Every Word You Say," the fourth selection of the second set, is a tune that I can usually skip, but on this night, Garcia's sculpting masterpieces. Sensitive singing and bubbly vocal inflections roll from Jerry on this Jesse Winchester love ballad. Musically, this song resembles the Grateful Dead's "It Must Have Been the Roses," except Garcia infuses "Every Word You Say" with a pair of intense solos. The second solo is manic, almost reaching the earlier majesty of "Tough Mama." The Great American Music Hall cuts loose with more thunderous applause, and they clamor for more.

The second set rolls on with Saunders' composition, "My Problems Got Problems," one of three songs that Merl sings this night. "I Feel Like Dynamite" and "Boogie on Reggae Woman" are the other two.

All three songs are long, funky, soulful, and executed with professionalism. However, I'm not enamored with Saunders deep, monotone voice. Legion of Mary's diversity is intriguing at times, but I also understand why Garcia felt like it might be time to move on to a new project.

In Blair Jackson's biography *Garcia, An American Life*, John Kahn stated that the band had reached a creative impasse: "It didn't seem to be headed anywhere for us....It was just a period of nongrowth musically, I thought, and Jerry thought so, too. We dealt with it like Jerry dealt with a lot of things—we just sort of ditched it. We just hid and just didn't have any gigs for a long time, and then we started another band."

Since their partnership began, Saunders' role in Jerry's bands had slowly expanded. They were never billed as the Jerry Garcia Band, but whatever name was put on it, Garcia was the Big Cheese, the larger-than-life attraction and creative force. But who can blame Saunders for seeking more action? It's a natural instinct for any talented musician in their prime. And Garcia was about as egoless as a rock star can be. He never wanted a leadership role, or the power that came with it. If unpleasant news needed to be passed on, Garcia avoided the hassle of being the messenger.

When Garcia and Weir traded songs on stage, it was part of the Grateful Dead chemistry, it all fit under the umbrella—Weir's contributions were an essential part of the band's magic. Saunders' songs didn't seem to successfully co-exist with Garcia's songs. Legion of Mary always delivered quality musicianship, but the X factor wasn't there on Merl's tunes, or Fierro's solos. Fierro blew a funky sax, but his style didn't add to the musical tension—there was too much idle time in between Garcia's forays. The only sax man who really held his ground and pulled off compelling solos by Garcia's side was Branford Marsalis.

Following the Legion of Mary breakup, Garcia and Kahn joined forces with the Keith and Donna Band, and then they ended 1975 as the Jerry Garcia Band with the brilliant, all-world piano player, Nicky Hopkins. After a nineteen-month touring hiatus, the Grateful Dead resumed touring again in the summer of 1976, and as sure as the sun will shine, JGB was there to get their fair share of kicks in between Dead tours.

Legion of Mary opens this 4th of July show with a bang, playing King Floyd's "I Feel Like Dynamite." Saunders' prime time performance is an ideal way to ignite the Independence Day revelry. Tutt's staggered drumming imbues "Dynamite" with a funky New Orleans flavor. The next number, "Someday Baby," is as American as baseball, apple pie, or Watergate. It all began with Sleepy John Estes and his 1935 creation, "Someday Baby Blues." In 1955, Muddy Waters recorded "Trouble No More," an adaptation of "Someday Baby Blues." The Allman Brothers turned a new generation on to "Trouble No More" on their eponymous debut album and *Live at the Fillmore East*. Garcia and Saunders exercised their inalienable American right to reinvent by playing "Someday Baby" on *Live at Keystone*. Garcia's interpretation suits my tastes; it's got that right blend of California Cool and torrid Delta Blues. However, this Legion of Mary version is somewhat passive—the band whistles a mesmerizing groove, yet there's not much bite to the leads. It's a home-town show, and Garcia's limbering up.

This must have been a very rewarding for night for Garcia personally. A year later he would celebrate America's Bicentennial with JGB by playing in the Great American Hall again. San Francisco's grandest nightclub, the Great American Music Hall, is an exquisite venue, with towering marble columns and ornate balconies, built in the aftermath of the 1906 San Francisco earthquake, and first opened as Blanco's. From 1907 till it was shut down in 1933, during the Great Depression, Blanco's was a restaurant/bordello—a freewheeling house of hedonism. Blanco's became The Music Box burlesque hall. In 1936, infamous burlesque dancer and actress Sally Rand purchased The Music Box. After a tempestuous twelve-year run, the place changed ownership and opened as Blanco's Cotton Club, a jazz joint that was San Francisco's first desegregated club. This establishment only lasted a few months. After a few name changes and two of decades of failed experimentation, a fire nearly wiped this historic landmark off the map. After it was rescued and fabulously refurbished, the Great American Music Hall was opened in 1972.

Garcia played in the Great American Music Hall thirty times: twenty-nine shows with Garcia-related configurations, and once with the Grateful Dead on August 13, 1975, a historic show featuring the debut of Help on the Way > Skipknot! > Franklin's Tower. The concert was released, years later, as *One From the Vault*. Surprisingly, the Jerry Garcia Band would never perform at the music hall again after 7-4-76. This was exactly the type of venue Garcia had a fondness for. The joint was laden with aesthetic charm, and haunted by an arcane past.

Legion of Mary lifts the music to higher ground with the third number of the night, "That's All Right Mama." Kahn opens with a bluesy bass rift similar to the one he plays in "That's What Love Will Make You Do." The band displays their diversity on three distinctive instrumentals that explore elements of blues, jazz, and rock. The pace isn't as relentless as most "That's All Right Mama" assaults, but the flawless musical navigation is special. If you crave a blistering guitar solo, the third one is wicked—another sublime flash of inspiration from Garcia on Independence Day.

On the heels of "That's All Right Mama" comes a "Mississippi Moon" that's as mellow as it gets. The music actually ceases for five seconds before Jerry belts out the chorus—complete silence! It's a lovely lullaby that only a Garcia enthusiast could enjoy. Don't try turning your heavy metal friends on to this one. "Mississippi Moon" went through a successful metamorphosis in the early '80s when Garcia added a fetching chord riff that made the arrangement more substantial. One of the biggest differences between the Grateful Dead and Garcia Band was how the songs progressed through the years. A lot of Grateful Dead numbers like "Tennessee Jed" and "Wharf Rat" became slower and slower, and seemed to decay from indifference. On the other hand, most JGB jingles were on the rise as the band stormed through the early '80s.

Legion of Mary ends the first set of 7-4-75 with a lengthy "Boogie On Reggae Woman." The band takes Stevie Wonder's marvelous tune and turns it into a superfluous marathon. There's a difference between covering songs in a professional manner, and glorifying them. Garcia had the gift of glorification, the ability to magnify and embellish a cherished melody, shining a light on it until he exposed a new truth within—owning the song and paying homage to it at the same time. When I listen to Saunders' remake of "Boogie on Woman," I long for Stevie Wonder's version.

One of Garcia's finest vocal presentations of the night is on the first encore, "It's Too Late." A blues ballad from Jerry's wonder years, "It's Too Late," was written and performed by Chuck Willis. Most classic rock fans discovered "It's Too Late" on Derek & the Dominoes' *Layla and other Assorted Love Songs*, where it's sensationally sandwiched between "Little Wing" and "Layla." Garcia sings this one with all the heartache he can bear to summon. Like "Someday Baby," "It's Too Late" was recorded for *Live at Keystone*.

An eighteen-minute "The Harder They Come" is the final notch on the belt of another epic Legion of Mary expedition. Thanks to three masterpieces: "Tough Mama," "That's All Right Mama," and "Every Word You Say," and the shifting, swirling magpie of Americana, this experiment in the Great American Music Hall lives as an artistic testament to the grand improviser, the storyteller from the streets of San Francisco, one of the last authentic Western heroes, Jerry Garcia.

6

11-4-81 ALBANY

RISE OF THE EAST COAST DEADHEAD

I can't recall how I celebrated my eighteenth birthday, an occasion that gave me the legal right to purchase alcohol in New York State, but on that very same day there was a jubilant celebration in the state capital, at Albany's Palace Theatre, where the Jerry Garcia Band and his rowdiest devotees were entrenched in a charged exchange of energy, emotion and devotion. Two nights later, on 11-6-81, I saw my first JGB gig at the Capitol Theatre in Passaic, New Jersey. I went on to have an illustrious career of following the JGB. My only regret is that my JGB journey didn't begin on 11-4-81.

A two-hour drive up the New York State Thruway separates my hometown of Nanuet from Albany. If I'd made the journey and arrived at the Palace Theatre fifteen minutes late, I wouldn't have missed much. Garcia's solos on "How Sweet It Is" and "Catfish John" are truncated. If the Music Mountain versions of these songs would rank a 10 out of 10 on an imaginary jam-o-meter, then the Albany "How Sweet It Is" gets a 2.5, and "Catfish John" a 4. It sounds as if Garcia's suffering from tour lag. It must have been a bumpy bus ride from his gig the night before in

Owings Mills, Maryland. Whatever the case may be, there is no fire in the belly of the beast early on in Albany.

As Garcia strums the climactic finale of the "Catfish John" jam, the Palace Theatre erupts. These overly eager fans are cuckoo for Jerry from the first note. Finally, they have a slab of filet mignon, and they crave more. Most of these hipsters are rabid Deadheads who attend college at SUNY Albany, or one of the plethora of upstanding schools in the area. One day they'll be the doctors, lawyers, scientists, and politicians of America, but on this night they are boisterous, stoned, Garcia-loving sycophants, escaping the cultural doldrums of the times—new wave, punk, Jordache Jeans, and *The Dukes of Hazzard*. For one night, their hero and fearless leader is blessing their adopted turf, and they are determined to make Mr. Garcia feel their love.

East Coast Deadheads inspired Garcia by raising a ruckus—hooting and hollering at exactly the right moments. These rowdy cats appreciated the intricacies of improvisation, and Garcia would respond by dialing up the jam—impassioned fret work. Garcia was the embodiment of California culture, yet his creativity thrived in the chaotic environments hovering around New York City, New Haven, Boston, and Philadelphia. The East Coast was fertile ground for the breeding of a new generation of Deadheads, and Jerry and The Boys had been planting seeds and rotating venues for several seasons.

In May 1977, the Grateful Dead rampaged through one of their greatest four-show runs, performing at the New Haven Coliseum (May 5), Boston Garden (May 7), Barton Hall, Cornell University (May 8), and the Buffalo War Memorial Auditorium (May 9). Their September 3 show at the Englishtown Raceway in New Jersey, in front of 100,000 fans, was arguably their finest performance of the year. And they followed that up by blowing away the college kids of New York, again, at Colgate, Rochester, and Binghamton on successive nights in November. Combining college gigs with big city gigs was a winning ticket, since the band rarely repeated songs at successive shows, and one concert is never enough for an impressionable, young Deadhead. A motivated fan wouldn't have to travel too far to catch a slew of shows. And with a transient college population migrating to and from the cities, the buzz spread—and so did the bootleg tapes. When the Grateful Dead were resting up, the Jerry Garcia Band was out there sowing the fields. This 11-4-81 show is JGB's fifth performance at Albany's Palace Theatre since 1977, and the audience is having multiple orgasms during every song, even if there's no reason to get excited.

JGB comes alive during an uplifting cover of Smokey Robinson's "I Second That Emotion." It's the sweet kiss that Albany craves. Garcia channels Smokey's sugary sentiments as the band lays down a melody riff that sounds like: "Bring out your dead, bring out your dead...Bring out your dead, babe... Bring out your dead, bring out your dead...Bring out your dead, babe." Julie Stafford and Liz Stires solidify the chorus harmonies. In addition to Kahn, Seals and Warren are handling the keyboard duties, and Ron Tutt is drumming. With the exception of Tutt, this is the same band that took the stage at Music Mountain.

Seizing the initiative, Garcia pokes the hornet's nest with "Mystery Train," a turbocharged bolt of King Elvis. In a few songs Garcia goes from sleeping giant to sizzling maestro. Jerry and his fanatical kingdom are now riding the same wave of ecstasy. It's an eight-and-a-half minute elbow-flapping, high-stepping, highfalutin good time. "Mystery Train" is the transformative performance, the one that really hurtles this performance towards immortality.

The set slams shut with "Deal." Once upon a time, this was a one-jam pony with a tight instrumental tucked in the middle; but now there's an outrageous ending jam, one that Garcia has been cultivating for the past year. The time has come for Garcia to take these SUNY students on a field trip through time and space to test out theories of sonic reality. But these kids are no fools; they've spent time in their quads and dorms studying bootleg tapes and preparing for this night. Maybe *they'll* be the ones pushing Garcia's buttons.

If there's a guitar solo that might tickle the fancy of a Clapton or Van Halen fan who has yet to appreciate the joys of Garcia,

I recommend the final solo from the Albany "Deal." Garcia opens swiftly with screeching twangs that'll burn your brain right out. The crowd is overwhelmed, and the crazed shouting begins: "Yeee-who-who-Yowwww!" "Garcia is god!" The illustrious Palace Theatre becomes the sight of a supernatural exchange between artists and audience. Garcia's charging hard, perhaps so much so that he will climax prematurely. Abruptly he steps out of that trap and redirects the course of the jam.

The music thunders. Kahn and Tutt are the sound and the fury—the Palace walls are shaking. A crazed outburst from Garcia draws a tumultuous roar—hound dogs on helium. Garcia restates the riff, louder, and with more authority. A wave of approval reverberates through the faithful, and the crowd barks for more: "Hit us again, O Great One!" An obliging Garcia drops the hammer—same melody line in a higher register, and incrementally quicker, 85 mph…90 mph…95 mph. Feeding off the loudest roar of the night, Garcia invents exclamation notes born out of the heat of the moment. It's an inspired collaboration, an emotional give and take between a performer and an audience in peak states, creating the type of music that can't be simulated in a sterile studio environment. Garcia would play many longer versions of "Deal" featuring mind-bending jams executed with brilliant technique; but few are as stunning as 11-4-81. There's virtuosity within this solo, but the real thrill is hearing how Garcia works the crowd, and how he lets the crowd work him. It's a time out of mind moment, aural transcendence captured on an audience recording. A soundboard recording wouldn't do this justice.

During intermission, I wonder if Garcia took a few moments to ponder his wanderlust, where he had been, and where he would be going as the year concluded. More than a long strange trip, Garcia's travels in 1981 were pure madness of an unprecedented nature. It all began in January, with a JGB West Coast tour. In February, JGB barnstormed intimate venues on the East Coast before swinging back to San Francisco for three shows. Frequent flyer points were accumulating. The Grateful

Dead tour commenced with three nights in Chicago at the end of February, and March began with two dates in Cleveland, followed by a short East Coast tour that ended in Hartford. The Dead then flew across the Atlantic for four shows in England, and one with The Who in West Germany. These were their first European appearances in seven years. When they returned to the Bay Area, Garcia slacked off a little by only scheduling five JGB gigs for April. Then the Dead headed east for their annual spring tour in May, and JGB closed the month with a West Coast run. Then Garcia slacked off again, only performing three JGB shows in June.

In July (by the way, we're still talking about 1981), the Grateful Dead rolled through a Midwest tour, and for good measure, the JGB crew played a few more in California. Between August and the middle of September, Jerry lingered out west for two short runs with the Grateful Dead, and of course, JGB shows were sprinkled in before, after, and in between the Dead shows. As September rolled to its chronological conclusion, the Grateful Dead headed east for gigs in Lehigh, Buffalo, and Washington, DC.

Just as they had done in May, The Boys followed an East Coast swing with a European tour—déjà vu all over again. After playing in Amsterdam and Paris, the Grateful Dead ended their thirteen-show rendezvous in Barcelona, Spain, on October 19. It was the first and only time Señor Garcia played in the land of his ancestors.

Believe it or not, this was where the craziness kicks in. Six days after leaving Barcelona and traveling halfway across the globe, JGB put on a show at Keystone Palo Alto. Four days later, JGB schlepped their act back to the East Coast to launch a tour at the Tower Theatre in Upper Darby, Pennsylvania. After several triumphant performances, including the 11-4 Albany show, JGB closed the tour out with performances in Chicago (11-17) and Denver (11-19 + 20). Ten days later, the Grateful Dead were in Pittsburg to launch a seven-date tour of the heartland that ended in Des Moines, Iowa, on the 40th anniversary of the attack on Pearl Harbor. Before the band performed their annual New Year's run at the Oakland Auditorium, JGB would do three more gigs in the Bay Area.

I can't explain this ambitious and hectic touring agenda, but Garcia attempts to address the situation as he opens the second set in Albany:

"Money; who needs it? I live a life free and easy. A toothbrush in my hand. Let me be a traveling man. I'm a roadrunner, babe." Garcia loves the life he lives, and he lives the life he loves.

Despite the intermission, JGB and their noisy disciples pick up where they left off. The band is hammering the groove. The velocity and vigor of "Roadrunner" is surreal. There's a brief keyboard interlude, but Garcia's guitar shredding dominates the action; ideas streaming freely—electrified Django Reinhardt. There was an awareness in the air that there were tapers capturing this piece of JGB history, and one day soon, these yodeling Garcia fanatics will be gathering friends in their dorms to turn them on to the bootlegs of this show. Sure there were a lot of people just tripping and enjoying the moment, but many Deadheads understood that they were witnessing something unforgettable, music that would thrive and grow in stature long after JGB left the Palace Theatre.

There's a rapturous response as Garcia's strings introduce the next song. Each thrilling note cuts through the smoky marijuana haze, and step by step, the music ascends like royalty floating towards Heaven. From his pulpit in the sky, Garcia's soul is exposed as the faithful cling to every word that the Bearded One weeps:

> I turn and walk away
> then I come round again
> It looks as though tomorrow
> I'll do very much the same
>
> I must turn down your offer
> but I'd like to ask a break
> You know I'm ready to give everything
> for anything I take

Fabulous allusion! The words are at the same time personal and universal. "Mission in the Rain" is Hunter's portrait of Garcia when they both resided in the Mission District of San Francisco. Garcia's wistful voice bubbles with deep feeling, as if he's singing about a past experience that's oddly become symbolic of his life. The passion of giving everything for anything one might take sums up the moment at hand. Garcia is giving up everything, including his physical and mental health, to bring righteous music to his fans. His zealous admirers are temporarily giving up everything they have to be here—college exams, day jobs, responsibilities be damned. The unbreakable bond and sacred communication between the performer and the audience is as intangible as it is immense; thousands of souls side by side, sharing an experience through the prisms of their own island universes.

There's a tension-filled pause in the music after the opening verse. An emotional chill rips through the Palace Theatre. Those who aren't choked up howl as Garcia continues to share Hunter's reflections. "Mission in the Rain" along with "Comes a Time" are the Hunter/Garcia gems from the aptly named *Reflections* (1976). Emotions continue to boil as Garcia sings:

Ten years ago I walked this street
my dreams were ridin' tall
Tonight I would be thankful
Lord, for any dream at all

Some folks would be happy
just to have one dream come true
but everything you gather
is just more that you can lose

"Mission in the Rain" was a moving anthem when it was debuted, but now, with Garcia closing in on his 40th birthday, you can hear him yearning for an earlier time when there was endless optimism and his dreams were riding tall—something better than the here and now, as cool as this might be. As we grow older and our capacity to dream diminishes, hopefully we become wiser. Garcia truly understood that "Everything you gather is just more that you can lose." Garcia had lost a lot during the last decade. His bushy black mane and beard had grayed prematurely, and his addiction to smoking Persian had him by the balls. But, all things considered, he still looked somewhat healthy, especially if you compare this Jerry to the ghastly, obese version of 1983. Maybe that's what makes this version so intense. Garcia could run and hide from the truth in his personal life, but as he croons "Mission in the Rain," he acknowledges that time is the enemy—it's all slipping away before our eyes.

With expressive and cascading guitar runs, Garcia evokes the pains and pleasures of the human experience as the band backs him in a dreamlike trance. Jerry's endless devotion to learning and practicing guitar scales shines through. We can all be thankful that when Garcia received an accordion for his fifteenth birthday, he swiftly traded it in for an electric guitar. In the Albany "Mission," his Tiger guitar has the gift of gab as he scurries from scene to scene—everything's poignant and picturesque—brilliant brushstrokes galore. Garcia's phrasing is immaculate. Each riff is a clever idea, complete with its own zestful flavor and texture. There's a brief interlude from Seals, but Garcia's guitar won't be hushed. Just when you think the Bearded One has ended a phrase, he sneaks in a spine-tingling flurry, a little something for us elitists who think we've heard it all. And the way Garcia manipulates the silence is an art form within itself.

Touching down for the final verse, Jerry confesses, "All the things I planned to do I only did halfway." Wow. Could you imagine if Garcia did things three-quarters of the way? In spite of all we accomplish and all we do, most of us still travel with the baggage of regret, and the belief that somehow we're not fulfilling our purpose.

When Garcia growls, "There's some satisfaction in the San Francisco rain. No matter what comes down, the mission always looks the same," the Albany faithful howls in approval. You don't have to be a Californian to experience satisfaction in the San Francisco rain. Garcia places you in his shoes, out on the glistening, rain-soaked streets of San Francisco.

Here's a footnote for you: Garcia repeats the "Come again, Walking along in the mission in the rain" chorus five times instead of the usual four. Magnificence has its distinguishing characteristics, and there's nothing like a well-timed miscue. What Garcia does with this final jam is truly miraculous. In fact, November 1981 is the best month in "Mission" history. The outro solos are wild and lengthy, especially this one. These are guitar leads to die for; these are the Glengarry leads, and Garcia has been saving them for Albany. Khan, Seals, Tutt and Warren slam away with all their might. Garcia's all over the map, but his command is undisputed. An explosive outburst is succeeded by surges that are terrifying, hilarious, regal, smug, sentimental, and snarky. It's startling how Garcia connects it all. All the phrasing works inside the "Mission" framework, but each phrase seems distinctive from anything he's played before. And as always, whenever Garcia is in The Zone, it all balances out like an advanced mathematical equation, with the laws of momentum firmly in place. With a total length of fourteen minutes and fifty seconds, this is the longest "Mission in the Rain."

Momentum, sweet momentum. JGB has it, and the rowdy crowd helps them sustain it. After such an overwhelming display, on a another night, Garcia might have slowed things down with "Simple Twist of Fate" or "Russian Lullaby," but instead, he almost incites a riot by busting into "That's What Love Will Make You Do," an atypical pick for the third spot of the second set. When Garcia sings, "No matter how hard I fight it, baby, I'm still in love with you," the faithful rejoice. Kahn's un-flinching bass line rises, falls, and slithers—a magnet for Jerry's whirl-wind activities. Garcia is the squirrel, Kahn is the tree.

`Garcia finally dips inside his first slow ballad of the night, "The Night They Drove Old Dixie Down." The crowd cheers as if they've been waiting all night for Jerry to begin this serenade: "Virgil Kane is the name and I served on the Danville train." Judging by the audi-ence reaction, you'd think that Garcia just announced the repeal of the

Prohibition Act. In the heart of Yankee Land, a century after the Civil War, Professor Garcia engages his students in a gorgeous voice. These are the golden days of Jerry's singing, and this "Dixie" is precious. Ron Tutt adds a chilling touch to this version by striking up a military funeral procession beat.

Out of the final "Dixie" chorus, JGB blasts into "Tangled Up in Blue." A classic Band anthem precedes a classic Dylan anthem— American history and culture rolls into one. How fabulous is that ? *One and one is two...Two and two is four.* Garcia's vocal presentation here is more attentive and alive than it is on the mammoth Cape Cod version (5-28-83). I dig the backing harmonies provided by Stafford and Stires, "Tangled up in blue, yeah, tangled up in blue…tangled up in blue, yeah, tangled up in blue…" From the Great North woods to New Orleans, JGB always tears up for the final leg of "Tangled Up In Blue." This isn't as deliciously over-indulgent as Cape Cod, but there's still lots of meat shaking on the bone.

It was not uncommon, even on a blessed night, for JGB to split without an encore. There was no chance Jerry was sliding out the backdoor without playing an encore in Albany's Palace Theatre on 11-4-81. Garcia adds to the jubilee by offering up a "Sugaree" encore. A great version of "Sugaree" can last upwards of eighteen minutes. This one is intense and short, ten minutes in length; however, the very gesture of performing "Sugaree" is pure bliss for his boisterous flock. As Garcia bid farewell to Albany, I was celebrating my birthday at a local saloon, and my dreams were riding tall. I was two days away from my first rendezvous with the Jerry Garcia Band.

7

5-31-83 ROSELAND

WEST SIDE STORY

As JGB rolled into Manhattan on the last day of May 1983, Garcia was in the midst of a brilliant streak. From May 26 through June 6, JGB played a dozen shows, all of them smoking. I've already lavished praise upon the second date of this Northeast tour, 5-28-83 Cape Cod. Garcia's physical health may have been plummeting into a horrifying abyss, but as summer beckoned, Garcia found salvation in his virtuosity. His guitar ramblings on this tour rank right up there with the best of his Grateful Dead glory days. That's right; break out the tapes from December '71, September '72, November '73, June '74, and May '77. There's an uncanny tenacity to Garcia's playing during this JGB run that's almost scary. He poures his soul into these solos, as if they're his sole purpose for existence in this universe. I jam, therefore I am.

On the fifth night of this tour, Garcia brought the Right Stuff to the Roseland Ballroom, located on West 52nd Street in the heart of Hell's Kitchen. It was JGB's first Manhattan performance since they rocked the Palladium twenty months earlier. New York City was an endless source of inspiration and fascination for Jerry. Instead of feeling out of pace, and out of place, Garcia was in awe of its functional anarchy. In an interview with David Gans, Garcia said:

"When you go to New York City, you see a place that's basically not being governed, and it runs pretty well….When you're there, you have this feeling of out-of-controlness which is unreal, but it somehow works. All those people are able to exist as governments of one, and do business, play their games, whatever, on their own terms."

A horde of Deadheads, operating as governments of one within a collective brotherhood, convened on the Roseland's dance floor to welcome the arrival of Garcia and his entourage. The lights dimmed, and out popped the Bearded One, in jeans and a red T-shirt that clung to his fireplug physique. This was a shocking wardrobe development for diehards who were accustomed to the black T-shirt and jeans ensemble. Garcia fortified his red surprise by opening with "Rhapsody in Red."

Outside of recognizing "Rhapsody in Red" from the *Cats Under the Stars* album, this is fresh meat for most of those in the salivating audience. A classic rhythm and blues chord progression is embellished by Garcia's trademark "Rhapsody" jazz lick. It's a time warp—Chuck Berry meets Wes Montgomery on the stage of 3 Deuces, a hopping be-bop club on West 52nd Street that thrived during and after World War II.

I love to hear that rhapsody in red
It just knocks me right out of my head
Lifts me up here just floatin' around
Sends me way up and don't let down

It's rare that Garcia will charge his audience like a bull in heat at this early juncture of a show, but New York City is ready for the nitty-gritty, and turned up for heavy turbulence. With their powerhouse drummer Greg Errico hustling and shuffling the beat along, JGB is equipped to manhandle any ballroom. "Rhapsody in Red" rages with all the combustible, yet self-contained madness of a crosstown traffic jam. With

"Rhapsody in Red," Garcia and Hunter had composed an old-timey rocker on par with "Let it Rock," "Tore Up Over You," and "Mystery Train," yet it seeks to cover more terrain, it exudes shades of Irving Berlin, George Gershwin, and "The Bird," Charlie Parker.

Digging into the lighter side of the Garcia/Hunter songbook, a sprightly "They Love Each Other" has the dance hall swinging and swaying. When the Grateful Dead introduced this love ballad to the live rotation in 1973, it was a spunky concoction. Unfortunately, the song was dropped from the rotation, and a neutered, slower version returned in 1976. It was still enjoyable, but "They Love Each Other" had pretty much become another song filling up time in Grateful Dead first sets, a lot like "Little Red Rooster" or "Row Jimmy." Unless you were just struck by cupid's arrow, "They Love Each Other" was as stimulating as a Bill Clinton nominating speech.

Thanks in large part to Melvin Seals' funky organ grinding, JGB returns excitement to "They Love Each Other," and with a Sly & the Family Stone drummer sticking the beat, everyday New Yorkers are dancing to the music. Throw in the soulful harmonies of Jerry's new divas, Jaclyn and Dee Dee, and suddenly "They Love Each Other" bounces like a Spalding off a city stoop. On this steamy Manhattan eve, Deadheads are sweating in the sauna that is the Roseland, and Garcia's two-pronged solo squeezes them like a sponge. The first strike is a reconnaissance mission—Garcia zigs and zags this way and that way. Round two is a mad dash to paradise. It's the best Garcia solo I've ever heard on this song, with the possible exception of the one he would play the following night in the Roseland.

JGB keeps the mother rolling with "That's What Love Will Make You Do." Welcome to Garcia's adaptation of *West Side Story*. Out on the streets the pimps, prostitutes, police, hustlers, dealers, and cabbies run wild, but in the warm confines of the Roseland, it's a love supreme—Garcia and his devotees are huddled in front of the stage like hormone-driven teenagers at a high school dance. This scene has the primal passion of Maria and Tony embracing on a West Side balcony.

The love is unconditional and reciprocal. *If you ever need/ There's no limit to what I'll do/ Work eight days a week, baby/ And give it all to you.* Little Milton's 1972 recording of this song is an ode to the powers of sexual attraction. As Garcia performed "That's What Love Will Make You Do" over the years, the lyrics evoked new connotations for both Garcia and his fan base.

The circuitous heat rises as the jam takes form. Garcia lays down the melody and turns up the intensity with each pass. His tone is splendid here, as his guitar and amp ride the thin precipice between clean and distortion. It's another day, and Chez Garcia is baking another cake. The Japanese have a word for this seemingly effortless perfection: *shibumi*. John Kahn's an integral part of this effortless perfection as he leads his mates into the mid-jam boogie riff. His bass resounds with clarity and authority, so much so, that it could stand on its own as a musical score. Garcia's digging it, and he expresses his pleasure with a guitar tirade that stretches horizontally and vertically—long and flowing lines, like those materializing from a bebop sax player. And then comes one of those hang-onto-your-hat moments as Jerry blows the roof off the Roseland. His stubby fingers are a-blur as he swings with the grace of a trapeze artist. The crowd goes berserk as Garcia picks his way to the zenith of all climaxes. *Shibumi!*

That's a show. Garcia could have sung a round of "And We Bid You Goodnight," tossed a handful of magic dust into the air, and waddled off stage. Instead, he plays "Valerie" and "How Sweet It Is" back to back, continuing with his Broadway adaptation of *West Side Story*. "Valerie" is a desperate plea of devotion to a two-timing woman, and "How Sweet It Is" is an idyllic love hymn, or, in this context, another confirmation of the bond between the band and their adoring patrons. "Valerie" contains a gritty blues jam, and "How Sweet It Is" comes off like a fluttering knuckleball in an uncustomary lineup slot.

"Run for the Roses" closes the opening Roseland set. It was a logical choice—save the big guns for later—*all good things in all good time*. "Run for the Roses" and "Touch of Grey" are Garcia/Hunter collaborations that appeared on the scene around the same time. I hear these tunes as twins—they sound similar, and both seemed destined for notoriety. Jerry rushed "Run for the Roses" on to the ill-fated album of the same name, while "Touch of Grey" landed in the Grateful Dead rotation, where it aged like fine wine. Following Garcia's coma, the band recorded "Touch of Grey" for *In The Dark* (1987). "Touch of Grey" went on to be a blockbuster, while "Run for the Roses" slid into obscurity. If I had to choose between the musical siblings, I prefer "Run for the Roses." This number would have thrived in the Grateful Dead rotation, and it could have been a nice addition to *Built To Last*, the Dead's disappointing follow-up to *In the Dark*.

The whole debate on why the Grateful Dead could never capture their sound in the studio can at times be tedious, so I'll share just a few thoughts on the matter. The band's greatest commercial success, *In the Dark*, achieved platinum status. For the recording sessions, the Grateful Dead set up on stage as if they were playing a live concert, and taped *In the Dark* with mobile recording equipment. This was a brilliant concept that produced wonderful results. Unfortunately, the songs of *In the Dark* don't capture the true improvisational nature of the band's music. *In the Dark* contains tasty guitar work, but it lacks a truly breathtaking or transcendental moment. What we have here are seven songs of Grateful Dead mediocrity at their best. "Black Muddy River," "West L.A. Fadeaway," and "Touch of Grey" are terrific songs, but nowhere on this album are there any jams bordering on epic. *American Beauty* and *Workingman's Dead* are stocked with better tracks, but once again, the immortal jam is missing in action.

Recording studios were like kryptonite to Garcia. Sure he could add tasty pedal steel guitar licks to "Teach Your Children," and contribute professionalism to any sessions, but he was a caged beast in the studio, where he was busy role-playing and fussing with gadgets. Garcia's essence thrived in his natural live environment, where there were few physical or mental barriers restricting time and space—his creative ideas could flourish. Garcia never craved commercial success, and he wanted to sidestep all the demands and hassles attached to it. On some subconscious level, I think Garcia sabotaged, or at least withheld, his best in the studio. How else could somebody explain *Run for the Roses*, a seven-song debacle with insipid versions of "Knockin' on Heaven's Door" and "I Saw Her Standing There." Garcia's previous release with the Grateful Dead, *Go To Heaven* (1980), was another bust, even though songs like "Alabama Getaway" and "Feel Like a Stranger" soared in concert. Clark Kent in the studio and Superman on stage, Garcia could eviscerate the memory of any studio schwag with one mighty live performance.

Kicking off set two with "The Harder They Come," JGB transforms the Roseland into a dancing, raving, madhouse that hadn't been seen in these parts since Studio 54 was closed down two years earlier. The band lays down a liberating groove that sets bodies spinning—one of those moments when JGB perfectly syncs themselves to the rhythms of the universe. Garcia's doing his thing, but this is a definitive jam for the band as a whole. Seals is in candy land, and the band feeds off his playful fantasies. The funky reggae shuffle in the middle is that patented JGB boogie-down, and Lord have mercy, it's better than ever. Hippie Samba dancing sprouts across the ballroom as the more vocally inclined New Yorkers holler boisterous encouragement at the band. For fifteen and a half minutes, pure revelry fills the air. Natural rhythms baste in their own juices, yet there's a midtown urgency to it all. This should be part of the mandatory curriculum for all Music Appreciation 101 classes.

It's amazing how Garcia seamlessly delivers these diverse ethnic influences to his predominately white audiences. If an artist is insincere, this kind of thing can backfire and come off as pretentious. But in Garcia's case, he puts his soul on the line, and recycles the music with extreme desire. No one digs a copycat, unless he's clever.

"Mission in the Rain" ensues. Everyone in the Roseland is thrilled; however, this pales in comparison to the 11-4-81 Albany coronation. The beat's too quick, and possibly Errico is at fault here, but it sounds like Jerry is emotionally detached, as if the lyrics are too personal for him to invest his heart and soul. This performance is as good as any other from this tour, but Garcia would never again lay it on the line like he did in November of 1981. Such is the ebb and flow of songs in the rotation of an inspired artist.

On my rich bootleg tape of 5-31-83, as "Mississippi Moon" begins, a rugged-sounding New Yorker bellows, "I love you, Jerry; I love you too, John." I too love Jerry and John, and I love this audience recording. Hearing these spontaneous outbursts helps place the listener on the packed dance floor. You can envision this lumbering guy with a beer swaying in his hand, howling his affections for JGB, and when the band nails a jam, you can feel the audience's explosion. I appreciate the cleanliness of soundboard recordings, but nothing tops robust audience tapes, and no fan base perfected the art of taping like Deadheads. After our friend's declaration of love for Jerry and John, a fetching "Mississippi Moon" intro slowly rises and falls:

A plinkity-plinkity-plink...ahh-plinkity-plinkity-plinkity-plink...
A plinkity-plinkity-plink...ahh-plinkity-plinkity-plinkity-plink.

Seals, Kahn, and Garcia have finally established the ideal sound for this whisper of a ballad. The music's inviting and evocative. You're on the porch rocking on a chair and hitting on a corncob pipe; and gazing into the starry skies, all you see is the big ol' Mississippi moon—its radiant glow reflects off the swamp below. When Jerry begins to croon, his voice is cranky, and he fumbles the lyrics, but his spirit bursts through any vocal hindrances. As he croons the chorus, you just want wrap your arms around the big guy and hug him. "Oh, Corey, I'll be coming soon/ From the Louisiana pines to the Mississippi Moon."

Garcia's heartfelt vocal inflections highlight the second verse. Many of my favorite Garcia vocal offerings are from this period, when he first began to struggle with his singing on a regular basis. When his voice sputters, as it does on this night, Garcia has to dig down deep and bypass his smoke-scarred throat with pure desire. And when he succeeds, as he does on "Mississippi Moon," there's a heroic flavor to it. His once reliable singing became a crapshoot, but at times, it's better than ever. When Garcia croons, "Honey, lay down beside me, angels rock us to sleep," there isn't a dry eye in the Roseland. It would take a cold, cold heart to not be moved by this poignant lullaby.

"Mississippi Moon" was written by Peter Rowan, Garcia's former Old & in the Way band mate, and the gentleman who also penned "Midnight Moonlight." When Rowan was in a band called Seatrain, they recorded "Mississippi Moon" for their third album, *Marblehead Messenger*. You have to respect an album named *Marblehead Messenger*.

Shifting from Rowan to Dylan, Garcia slams into "Tangled Up in Blue," but unfortunately, Garcia's gassed. His voice has all but given out on him, and the main guitar solo lacks length and passion, especially when compared to the epic Cape Cod version three nights earlier.

I propose that if Garcia were anywhere but New York City, he might have called it a night. With outstanding versions of "They Love Each Other," "That's What Love Will Make You Do," "The Harder They Come" and "Mississippi Moon" in the bank, this show was like no other. Yet, this was 1983, and Garcia had rediscovered the joys of playing songs from *Cats Under the Stars*. How could Garcia pass on playing "Gomorrah" in New York City? Times Square was raging in all its sleazy glory, and the Westies, a bloodthirsty Irish gang, were chopping up their victims' body parts and floating them down the East River. Mayor Koch was gorging himself with gargantuan pastramis on rye, and in a whiny voice asking everybody, "How am I doing?" When Garcia sings, "Don't you turn around, no, don't look after you. It's not your business how it's done you're lucky to get through," it pretty much sums up a normal day in Manhattan. If these were ancient times, the Lord would have blown the Big Apple off the map for numerous counts of reckless immorality. As for Garcia's band, they deliver a gripping biblical account of "Gomorrah," and Jaclyn and Dee Dee chime in with spirited gospel harmonies.

Garcia then asks all the sinners to step forward and testify by shimmying to "Deal." *Don't you let that deal go down.* It's as if Garcia's telling his hedonistic flock not to give up on their evil ways just yet. "Deal" closes the set, but Garcia's solo fizzles. Some Garcia enthusiasts might listen to this "Deal" and think my criticism is overly harsh, but the Roseland "Deal" from the following night blows it away. It's longer, more intense, and darkly driven. The entire 6-1-83 show is immense, on par with this one. On 6-1-83 Garcia's the devil in a black T-shirt; on 5-31-83 he's an angel in red. Take your pick. Opening night at the Roseland ends with a "Midnight Moonlight" encore, completing a wild thirteen-song affair. Jerry will be back in black to settle all scores at the Roseland in less than twenty-four hours. Sweet dreams, Gotham.

Grizzly Garcia and Kahn at the Roseland Ballroom, 1983. ©Bob Minkin

8

JAILHOUSE BLUES UNPLUGGED

Bob Dylan married Isis on the fifth day of May, and Jerry Garcia and John Kahn played an acoustic gig for an intimate gathering of inmates at the Oregon State Penitentiary on Cinco de Mayo, 1982. During the Grateful Dead's 1980 residencies at the Saenger Theatre (New Orleans), Warfield Theatre (San Francisco), and Radio City Music Hall (New York), the band opened each show with an acoustic set. Arista Records released a superb compilation of acoustic numbers from Radio City and the Warfield on the double album *Reckoning*, an endearing slice of Americana, and a reminder to infidels that magic was still stirring in the Grateful Dead tank.

As for the solo career of Garcia, 1982 marked his first extended acoustic run since his Old & in the Way days. In lieu of another JGB tour, Garcia scheduled acoustic gigs during and after the Grateful Dead's Northeast spring fling. The debut acoustic show was at Garcia's East Coast stomping ground, the Capitol Theatre in Passaic, New Jersey, on 4-10-82. Garcia appeared solo…no Kahn! The tapes reveal a confident performer holding the show together with cagey strumming, buttery leads, and peak vocals, but Garcia felt uncomfortable and incomplete.

He asked Kahn to join him with a standup bass at the next show, eleven nights later at the Beacon Theatre. Kahn and Garcia together forever. A few weeks later, the dynamic duo would face a roomful of Oregon felons and attempt to soothe their savage souls with sweet serenades.

Live at Folsom Prison begins with a masculine voice greeting the inmates, "Hello. I'm Johnny Cash." The Man in Black injects himself into the prison experience with gritty versions of "Folsom Prison Blues" and "Dark as a Dungeon." It's unlikely that Garcia, The Buddha in Black, introduced himself to the jailbirds. Our soundboard recording of 5-5-82 commences with the sweet twangs of the second solo of "Deep Elem Blues," a scrappy old timey traditional tune that had to resonate with the prison population, especially when Garcia sings about paying off the man: "Have your twenty dollars ready when that old policeman comes." Inflation strikes again. When Garcia sang this in 1970, the appropriate bribe was ten dollars. The first two verses are cut, but that's all right because "Deep Elem Blues" was Garcia's standard acoustic opener—there's plenty more where that came from. Hearing the recording begin with Garcia's solo in midflight is a charming attribute of this tape that's a staple in many Garcia bootleg collections.

"Add a little more guitar would you…yeah, that's it," says Garcia. Listening to this soundboard, we have the privilege of eavesdropping on between-song banter. Garcia slides into "Friend of the Devil," and the inmates howl as they name that tune. Cash's iconic Folsom Prison performance was a blatant address to his captive audience, while Garcia's set communicates similar sentiments in subtle fashion. Garcia gently sings, "The sheriff's on my trail/and if he catches up with me I'll spend my life in jail." Those words come across in a way they never had before—incarcerated men are wistfully looking back on their final days of freedom.

Garcia and Kahn intertwine on a stunning instrumental. They solo simultaneously with no rhythm holding things together, but they know each other and the "Devil" terrain so well that the jam molds into an absolute wonder of creation, a must-hear conversation—snapping guitar strings anchored by bubbling bass burps. There's a sad, regretful tone here, as if Garcia and Kahn are tapping into all the dark and · lonely nights of despair that have been spent inside this creepy institution. I don't think Garcia put much conscious thought into playing a set of music for an incarcerated crew, it's just that his standard acoustic songs speak the language of the outlaw, and they tell the tales of the dispossessed.

The "Friend of the Devil" from *American Beauty* is an anomaly. It's unusual that any folk-styled song receives its due on FM radio, but this is a blessed tune. The Grateful Dead restructured "Devil" for the live electric format, but the versions from 1972 through 1974 didn't have the same charisma as the original. Garcia radically restructured "Devil" in '75, transforming it into a tender ballad that was played occasionally by JGB for a few years. For the Grateful Dead, the mellower "Devil" went on to become a customary first set inhabitant. In essence, Garcia did unto his composition as he did unto other's compositions. By slowing the "Devil" down, Garcia magnified and savored the beauty within his tune. All the "Devil" reincarnations are effective on some level; electric or acoustic, fast or slow. This melancholy rendition from the Oregon State Penitentiary ranks up there with the best of them.

After "Devil," Jerry concedes, "That was good. Let's see." Garcia treats the boys in the pen to "Jack-A-Roe," a spirited sea shanty. This ditty, about a girl who dresses as a sailor to find her lost love, made its Grateful Dead debut in Chicago on 5-13-77. Garcia's perky interpretation of this traditional folk ballad makes it successful in either an acoustic or electric format. Facing the inmates, Garcia and Kahn weave acoustic magic. Kahn's bass bull-rushes ahead as guitar twangs gracefully skate along. Garcia keeps the traditional ballads rolling with "Oh Babe, it Ain't No Lie," a song that is sometimes credited to Elizabeth Cotton. The melody is pretty and hypnotic as Garcia whisper/sings the lyrics. It's the type of tune that sucks my mind into a trance—in one instant I'm admiring Jerry's talents, and then I'm completely zoned out, just pondering the daily minutia of existence. "Oh Babe, it Ain't No Lie" is a stoic piece, as even-keeled as it gets for Garcia.

Out of the silence that follows, an eager audience member yells out something that sounds like, "Who ate the tigers?"

Garcia chuckles, ponders the request for a moment, and quips, "I haven't really got that together to do. I'm sorry. If I'd have known..." Garcia chatter is rare, but here we get a taste of his sardonic wit. This tape is loaded; every morsel is compelling.

From the bizarre realm of folk, Garcia and Kahn plunge into "It Takes a Lot to Laugh, It Takes a Train to Cry." "Who Ate the Tigers?" be damned! I dig the propulsion of an electrified "Train," but this performance is damn-near perfect. Garcia and Kahn seamlessly balance the tempos and melodies of Dylan's blues classic—the rhythm's unshakeable, and the solos scream as if Robert Johnson's blistered fingers are pinching the burning strings.

It sounds like Garcia has settled into this performance and this environment. It's not every day that he plays for confined desperados, and whatever weirdness he may have felt early on seems to be long gone. Momentum is on the rise as Jerry shoots into "Run for the Roses." Within this stripped-down acoustic arrangement, Hunter's lyrics really sparkle.

Run for the rose, get caught on the briar
You're warming to love, next thing there's a fire
You got the do re, I got the mi
And I got the notion, we're all at sea
Yes, we're all at sea

Kahn leads the way into the chorus with a cluster bomb bass run. As Garcia sings "Run for the Roses" in the obscurity of an Oregon prison, horse racing fans braced for their Run for the Roses, the Kentucky Derby, which would take place in three days in Louisville. Gato Del Sol won the 1982 Kentucky Derby. I ask who among you will ever forget the moment that magnificent thoroughbred galloped across the finish line? Answer: almost everybody, including racing diehards. Thanks to a soundboard recording of 5-5-82, however, this show went from obscurity to immortality many years down the line. Nothing transcends time like great art.

Luckily, someone in Garcia's entourage patched a tape deck to the soundboard so that the show would eventually get around. I didn't get my hands on a copy of this soundboard until I purchased it at one of those record shops that carries bootleg CDs down on Bleecker Street. I was happy to part with twenty-five bucks to get this boot that was titled *Lonesome Prison Blues*. A few years later I discovered the budding audio downloading scene online; however, we tend to cherish things that we pay for more than freebies. I think it's fair to assume that no audience tapes of 5-5-82 exist. There must have been some Garcia enthusiasts in Oregon State Penitentiary, probably doing time for distribution or possession of narcotics. Sure, taping the gig would have been a bit of a hassle, although I wouldn't put it past a few determined Deadheads to conspire to sneak taping equipment in and out of the jail. Deadheads are ubiquitous: prisoners, guards, cooks, Mafioso...

Those prisoners with an appetite for the good ol' Grateful Dead unleash an elated roar when Garcia and Kahn segue from "Run for the Roses" into "Ripple." For studio underachievers, the Grateful Dead painted an eternal masterpiece with "Ripple." As Jerry's voice floats through the putrid air of this barbaric institution, fleeting optimism fills the hearts and minds of the prison population. If they could only find a way to bottle the warmth within Jerry's velvet tones and Hunter's poetic rhymes, their hard times might pass more peacefully. *Would you hear my voice come through the music? Would you hold it near as it were your own?* One of the irrefutable pleasures of seeing acoustic Garcia was the inevitability of hearing "Ripple," which he played at just about every show. That alone was always worth the price of admission. The best versions of "Ripple" were from the 1980 Grateful Dead acoustic sets. When

Bob Weir and Brent Mydland harmonized with Jerry, "Ripple" came off like a sacred hymn sung by a choir of angels.

Following a brief break, Garcia and Kahn return for more tales of temptation, retribution, redemption, violence and justice. "I've Been All Around This World" is the fourth traditional folk song of the show, and the bloodiest of the batch. Garcia sings, "Hang me, oh, hang me, so I'll be dead and gone. I wouldn't mind you hangin' boys, but you wait in jail so long." In the early nineteenth century, the state of Oregon used execution as a means to handle violent criminals prior to building the Oregon State Penitentiary in 1851. The days of hangings were long gone, but when Garcia and Kahn sang their songs, there were men in this prison languishing on death row. Like most American prisons, this gruesome place has a long history of inhumane treatment of inmates. In a 1968 riot, the prisoners took forty guards and employees hostage. In the aftermath of the uprising, the seventy-three year-old warden was relieved of his duties, but little was done to improve conditions. When Garcia sings, "Lulu, my Lulu, come and open the door. Before I have to walk on in with my old .44," he's addressing a group of men who understand all levels of violence. Even pets aren't immune from violence on this night. During "Valerie," the singer shoots his dog because the mutt had the gall to growl at the woman of his desire. He also slashes her lover, but he has just enough humanity to spare his life. "Valerie" fits right in with the bitch's brew of folklore conjured up on this evening.

As the set wraps up with "Dire Wolf," Jerry pleads, "Don't murder me, I beg of you, don't murder me. Please, don't murder me." Garcia sings of scenes that must have been tantalizing for the inmates—a card game around the fire with a bottle of red whiskey for supper. As I recall, "Dire Wolf" was the *Reckoning* track that received the most FM airplay when the album was released. I prefer the *Reckoning* "Dire Wolf" over the studio track on *Workingman's Dead*, largely due to Garcia's robust vocal effort. In a Robert Hunter journal entry dated 7-29-96, he discusses the birth of "Dire Wolf":

"The song "Dire Wolf" was inspired, at least in name, by watching the *Hound of the Baskervilles* on TV with Garcia. We were speculating on what the ghostly hound might turn out to be, and somehow the idea that maybe it was a Dire Wolf came up. Maybe it was even suggested in the story, I don't remember. We thought Dire Wolves were great big beasts. Extinct now, it turns out they were quite small and ran in packs. But the idea of a great big wolf named Dire was enough to trigger a lyric. As I remember, I wrote the words quickly the next morning upon waking, in that hypnogogic state where deep-rooted associations meld together with no effort. Garcia set it later that afternoon."

After a spirited stroll through "Dire Wolf," Garcia thanks the boys and is about to head backstage, or wherever a performer heads after a set of music in a state penitentiary. There are cries for one more. Garcia obliges.

"One more…Okay…This song's got a lot of words and I might not remember all of them."

Garcia went on to nail every word of the thrilling and rarely played "Reuben and Cerise," not that anyone holed up in the Oregon State Penitentiary would have known if he flubbed a verse or two, or had the wherewithal to hold him accountable. JGB had only played "Reuben and Cerise" live a handful of times around the release of *Cats Under the Stars* before shelving it until Garcia debuted an acoustic version at the Capitol Theatre on 4-10-82. "Ruben and Cerise" is the lovely opening cut of *Cats Under the Stars*. In the studio, Garcia begins singing each line with a breathy vocal inflection, a slick trick that fortifies a pleasurable track. And with this endearing jailhouse encore, Garcia sends the men off with a message they long to hear: "Goodnight and sweet dreams."

There's nothing like an acoustic "Reuben and Cerise." As Garcia and Kahn strum and thump away, a sprightly melody takes flight. A fleeting New Orleans love story unfolds with three-dimensional imagery: *Cerise was brushing her long hair gently down…Reuben was strumming his painted mandolin. It was inlaid with a pretty face in jade…The breeze would stop to listen in...The truth of love an unsung song must tell.* Hunter's musings suit Garcia's tastes; a place where fair maidens swirl to strings, and exotic rhythms flow in seductive and strange settings.

What should impress anyone who listens to this performance is Garcia's passion, which vibrates in every syllable emanating from his still-lively larynx. *If you can see my heart, you'd know it's true.* That's his distinction as a vocalist—other sensational singers sing with heart; Garcia sings directly *from* the heart, especially when he's exhaling Hunter's poetry. As the dynamic duo strum madly, they create a framework for the lush imagery that entangles sexual infatuation with music, sweet music. Garcia pushes his strings to the breaking point. After his axe withstands the final pounding, Jerry bids the boys farewell. "Thanks a lot. Thank you. It's been nice playing for you guys."

"Reuben and Cerise" was an ideal encore for a show dominated by six Garcia/Hunter compositions, even though it deviates from the desperado flavor of the set, and maybe because it does. If this performance were released, it would be Garcia's *Live at Folsom Prison. Garcia And Kahn Unplugged* would compare favorably to anything from the MTV *Unplugged* series. It's fifty-two minutes of intimacy with Garcia; everything's exposed. We even get to experience his wit and thoughts between songs. Garcia's voice has ripened into peak form; there's no wear and tear evident in this mellifluous presentation. It also stands as a phenomenal tribute to the lyrical prowess of Robert Hunter. These songs flow like fine wine and the buzz sneaks up on you. The allure of this gig grows with each listen; it ages gracefully, like an underrated Dylan album such as *Planet Waves* or *John Wesley Harding.*

With just Kahn by his side and an acoustic guitar in his hands, Garcia's anxiety and vital signs must have been off the charts as he began to perform for these cooped-up bandits, yet he swiftly acclimated to his environment and transferred the adrenaline rush into his performance. Johnny Cash was in his element performing in front of inmates, but this was way out of Garcia's comfort zone, although he shared a bond with this audience. You might ask, aside from performing outlaw ballads, what did Garcia have in common with these imprisoned thugs? Answer: everything. He never served any real jail time, but just being Jerry Garcia was an experience every bit as confining as a life sentence without parole. His Persian and heroin addictions turned him into a social leper. Outside of performing, Garcia's main interest was scoring junk, and he befriended an inner circle of confidantes who understood the trappings of a junkie's lifestyle, and were willing to join in, or look the other way. Garcia was also imprisoned by his celebrity. Phil Lesh, Bill Kreutzmann, and Bob Weir could roam city streets, at least briefly, without being mobbed by fans. There was only one dude who looked like the grandfatherly guru of the Grateful Dead. I've seen some elderly gentlemen with bushy beards who slightly resembled Garcia, but nobody who's seen the real deal could ever be fooled by an imposter.

This was Garcia's State of the Union Address to some of the most notorious criminals of the Pacific Northwest. What kind of dialogue might have taken place between Garcia and some of the prisoners if they'd had a chance to rap after the show? Your guess is as good as mine, but I think it might resemble something like what Dylan grumbled at the end of "Ballad in Plain D:"

Ah, my friends from the prison, they ask unto me
"How good, how good does it feel to be free?"
And I answer them most mysteriously
"Are birds free from the chains of the skyway?"

9

7-24-80 BUSHNELL

SUGAREE PSYCHOLOGY
& HISTORY 101

Home of the extravagant Bushnell Center for the Performing Arts, Hartford became the state capital of Connecticut in 1875. Many folks are also aware that Hartford is known as the "Insurance Capital of the World," but few realize that this metropolis of premiums and policies is also the "Sugaree Capital of the World." During a seven-year run, Garcia blessed Hartford with six mega-servings of the glorious guitar anthem that is "Sugaree." It all began in 1977, when "Sugaree," a formerly pleasant first set Grateful Dead tune, suddenly blossomed into a monster with three solos, with at least one of those solos being epic in magnitude. Perhaps the most ostentatious version of the year was served up inside the Hartford Civic Center on 5-28-77. A tradition was born. The Grateful Dead performed stunning "Sugarees" in the Hartford Civic Center on 3-14-81, 4-17-82, and 10-15-84. The Jerry Garcia Band helped bolster Hartford's "Sugaree" legacy with smoking renditions on 7-24-80 and 5-29-83 at the Bushnell. Fact: there are no killer "Sugarees" after Garcia's 1986 coma. He lost the ability, and or the desire, to pull off blockbuster "Sugaree" solos.

Hartford "Sugaree" fever spread to Connecticut's other primetime city, New Haven. On 6-17-82, JGB bounced a dynamic "Sugaree" off the walls of the New Haven's Veteran's Memorial Coliseum. In the same building, the Grateful Dead wowed their legion of fanatics with excellent versions on 10-17-82 and 4-23-84. Are all these Garcia guitar rampages merely a coincidence? I say not! I'll put forth the proposition that our boy, Jerry, consciously established song legacies in certain cities, states and venues. It also might be chalked up to a weird kind of déjà vu that snuck up on Garcia while he was on stage—vibrations and auras from performances past that never entirely left the arena, their presence lingered in the nooks and crannies of halls, stalls and rafters. Garcia had a cosmic sense of history and tradition. Whenever the Bearded One stepped on stage in Hartford or New Haven, a great "Sugaree" beckoned.

Enough of these history lessons. Let's switch the topic to "Sugaree" Psychology 101. Garcia opens the 7-24-80 Bushnell show with "Sugaree," a ballsy choice. Other standard openers like "How Sweet It Is," "I'll Take a Melody," and "Cats Under the Stars" were easier to pull off. If Garcia was off his game, not feeling it, or there were equipment issues, he could sail his way through one of these openers while he worked out the kinks. There's no place for refuge in "Sugaree." In between singing as sweetly as a robin, Garcia had to create and execute three fly-by-night solos that complement each other, a true test of his virtuosity. When Garcia opened with "Sugaree," pure adrenaline filled the building—you knew Garcia would try to knock your socks off, and inevitably, he'd succeed.

As an overly attentive fanatic, whenever I'd see a live "Sugaree" I'd prepare for a three-pronged attack. The opening solo of an ideal "Sugaree" should be playful, with a few sharp teases foreshadowing the madness to come. The ensuing guitar passage should be longer and more intense, with one or two climactic runs; yet Garcia should hold something back for the last solo. Sometimes, if the second jam was too climactic, Garcia pulled up lame in the third solo. But when Garcia orchestrates the "Sugaree" journey in an orderly manner, the third and final solo is a sensational blitz of tenacity and repetitious creativity. Garcia's fingers are a blur as he molests the fret board, top to bottom and back again. The overwhelming sonic wave tingles the brain as gravity pulls legs and arms and bodies and bones. There's no rush like it; that's why so many are hopelessly hooked on Garcia.

The Bushnell "Sugaree" has a perky opening solo. Ozzie Ahlers kicks off the second instrumental with a jarring synthesized keyboard run that's enthusiastically received. During "Sugaree," it's unusual for a keyboardist to step into the equation. You have to respect Ozzie's courage. This JGB quartet is almost the same as the one from the Oswego show (2-17-80). The only personnel change is Greg Errico replacing Johnny de Foncesca on drums. Spurred on by Ozzie, JGB closes out the instrumental with authority. The third solo is a speed picking fest—all scales, it lacks a dramatic flourish. Overall, the Bushnell "Sugaree" receives high marks, and the raucous crowd devours all the subtle twists and turns.

Garcia chases "Sugaree" with "That's What Love Will Make You Do." It's an exhilarating one-two punch, and a telltale sign of things to come. Errico's pummeling the drums aggressively, challenging Garcia and Kahn to step out. The sound is thicker than it was when the JGB quartet toured the East Coast in February, although that tour is legendary. Garcia follows with a clean performance of "Friend of the Devil," the complete antithesis of the sloppy 2-17-80 Oswego version. Once again, Errico's upbeat tempo influences the results. For my tastes, this is a tad faster than I like my "Devils," but I appreciate variety, and the instrumental comes alive with a danceable flow.

Garcia opts to slow the show down with "Simple Twist of Fate"; however, the hyper East Coast Heads reject that notion. They're a-hooting and a-hollering and inappropriately clapping along as Garcia wistfully winds down time. It's a moody and reflective piece that's not nearly as powerful or engaging as Dylan's version. As the dirge drags on, a Kahn bass solo looms. Garcia's singing is tender and true, but the overall effect of the song usually dulls the senses like a shot of heroin.

Yet there's a restless fever burning in the Bushnell. The out-of-place crowd clapping seems to sharpen Garcia's focus. His strings cry a shrill tale of solitude. Ahlers takes his turn and plunks some bluesy riffs. Bypassing a bass solo, Garcia picks up the baton and tears into the heart of the composition. When Garcia sings the final verses, his lonesome voice walks the razor's edge. The crowd's riled up as Garcia growls the final lines, "She was born in spring, but I was born too late. Blame it on a simple twist of fate. Blame it on a simple twist of fate. Wellll! BLAME IT ON A SIMPLE TWIST OF FATE!" JGB smashes and thrashes a succinct crescendo. This is another blatant example of how a high-stung East Coast audience influenced Garcia's performance, almost to the point of collaboration.

"Tangled Up in Blue" closes the set, and in the process, Garcia plays the first two tunes from *Blood on the Tracks* in reverse order. The Bushnell is buzzing; fans are hanging on to every Dylan phrase as Garcia embellishes the breadth of the lyrics with gregarious guitar sprints. Ahlers injects his passion for "Tangled Up in Blue" as the second instrumental begins, and Jerry's hot on Ozzie's tail, lashing out as if he's striking a piñata with a bullwhip. There's a short, intense ending jam, but "Tangled Up in Blue" is still in a state of becoming. In a year's time, the final jam ascended to epic proportions—*all good things in all good time.*

When the lights came on for intermission, the wild-eyed audience was faced with the sobering reality that they were in Hartford, a state capital with laws, regulations, and double indemnity policies, although, if there was a safe haven for hippie hedonism in Hartford, it was inside the magnificent art deco confines of the Bushnell Auditorium. After an hour of transcending with the JGB, content Jerry Heads could stare at the ceiling and admire "Drama," the largest hand-painted mural of its kind in America, and ponder what treats Garcia would dish out in the second set.

"I'll Take a Melody," "Sitting In Limbo," and "Russian Lullaby" are the first three items on the menu. These are insightful and calm ballads, and it's unusual that these songs would end up in the same show as "Friend of the Devil" and "Simple Twist of Fate." However, this is a performance where every song comes off, whether it's a whispering lullaby or a barnburner. When Garcia's in the zone, and he tunes his guitar just right, and finds those sweet spots and sounds that match his mood and vision, that show becomes an entity unto itself. When you listen to this tape, you can notice shared patterns of playing amongst these songs that are unlike any other show. Garcia's Bushnell forays feature garrulous phrasing that's melodious—a cool balance of passion and precision. And on this night, Garcia shows no favoritism; every song is precious, and every solo is handled with care.

The opening notes of "I'll Take a Melody" lightly touch down like leaves falling from trees. With Errico and Kahn prodding Garcia, the jam scoots along until a sonic vortex is formed. After the generous jam, "Melody" lands as elegantly as it began. Garcia croons, "I'd understand why the old sailor man, sail along, sail along, someday he'll be gone."

Before "Sitting Here in Limbo" takes flight, a misguided fan yells out some odd Grateful Dead requests, "The Wheel…Alligator!" Uh, not tonight, my friend.

"Russian Lullaby," a one-verse number penned by the incomparable Irving Berlin, was recorded by Garcia for *Compliments*, and it was added to the JGB rotation late in 1975. The overachieving Bushnell faithful are pumped as they clap along to this snail of a tune, just as they had during "Simple Twist of Fate." Jerry's voice is both plaintive and hopeful when he croons "Rock-a-bye my baby, somewhere there may be. A land that's free, for you and me. In a Russian Lullaby." This is the kind of lyric that Garcia covets—freedom from oppression inside an ordinary jingle. The band marches slow and steady, Jerry's fingers prance in between the body and the neck of his Tiger, spinning clusters of notes that pay homage to Mother Russia and the unyielding spirit of her people, past and present. The Soviet Union had just invaded Afghanistan, but that was the aggression of a Communist regime, not the will of the people. In the state capital of Hartford, JGB, perhaps the most diverse American band, thrilled a crowd of Yankee youth with a ballad that was as Russian as a bowl of borsht, and in the process, JGB transcended the politics of fear and loathing.

This show needs an amphetamine jolt, so Dr. Garcia prescribes the Sun Records scorcher, "Mystery Train." Kahn and Errico rev up a fuel-injected tempo. The propulsion of the jam is unreal; whiteout conditions exist as Garcia pumps out a blizzard of notes. One can only imagine the spastic dancing that must have been taking place in the aisles. No hippie is potentially as dangerous as a whirling, twirling, elbow-flapping freak topping off his or her routine with a 360-degree loop.

It's all just part of another night's work for. Garcia, who follows with "Mission in the Rain." Standing at the pulpit, Garcia pleads with the Almighty to keep hope alive: *Ten years ago I walked these streets/my dreams were ridin' tall/Tonight I would be thankful/Lord, for any dream at all.* The jam drives out lingering demons as the faithful sway to and fro. And like any preacher who been moved by the Holy Spirit, Garcia saves his evangelical crescendo for the finale. A sublime "Mission" guitar outro is essential to any memorable "Mission," and Garcia positively delivers here, triggering sensational leads rocketing with emotion... Hallelujah! Garcia punctuates the prayer with an intense chord-fanning dash across the finish line, and then releases the tension by galloping into "Midnight Moonlight. "Scoobie-doobie-doo, scoobie-doobie-doe... Scoobie-doobie-doo, scoobie-doobie-doe—*If you ever feel lonesome/ And you're down in San Antone/ Beg, steal or borrow two nickels or a dime/To call me on the phone/And I'll meet you at Alamo Mission/ We can say our prayers/ The Holy Ghost and the Virgin Mother/Will heal us as we kneel there.* Rolling thunder reverberates through the theatre. Joyous revelry ensues. The middle-aged madmen impose their will on the crowd. Dancers swirl, sway, and swing as bosoms bounce—chills and thrills fill the Bushnell. If JGB ever played a song with hit potential, "Midnight Moonlight" was that tune.

A night like this deserves an unforgettable send off, and Jerry complies with a "Dear Prudence" encore. Garcia performed his first "Dear Prudence" with Reconstruction on April 13, 1979 at the Rainbow Music Hall in Denver. Hearing JGB casually stroll into this Beatles *White Album* favorite is a rapturous experience for those in the Bushnell. Few people in the theatre are even aware that Garcia played "Dear Prudence," a song that was on its way to becoming an exotic JGB showpiece.

A Beatles reunion was a farfetched fantasy, but at least it was still a possibility in the summer of 1980. Sir Paul was still having his way with the American record-buying public. His live version of "Coming Up" was the number one song in the US for a few weeks as June turned into July. The studio version of that song is lame, a hint of things to come from Sir Paul in the early '80s, but I must confess my love for the released live version of "Coming Up" from Glasgow. Even John Lennon was inspired by that version. The hippie Beatle credited "Coming Up" as a motivating factor for him to get back to where he once belonged, in a recording studio. After a five-year recording hiatus, Lennon came out with *Double Fantasy*. By the end of the year, "Just Like Starting Over" was the number one song in America, although Lennon would never see that day. Three weeks earlier, he was gunned down in front of the Dakota, on the outskirts of Central Park West.

Talking about number ones, 7-24-80 was the twenty-fifth anniversary of the release of the number one song of all time, according to *Rolling Stone* magazine, Dylan's "Like a Rolling Stone." Those were the days, the summer of '65, when John, Paul, Dylan and Garcia were on their way, expanding the possibilities of music.

Imagine the joy inside the Bushnell when Garcia's voice took flight: "Dear Prudence, won't you come out to play? Dear Prudence, greet the brand new day-ay-ay-ayyyyyy." Since the Beatles never played a live "Dear Prudence," this must have been an immense experience. When "Back in the U.S.S.R." fizzles into "Dear Prudence" on the *White Album*, it's an incredible moment that's soothing and magical. The only regret I have with the Beatles version is that it's too fleeting. Obviously, time won't present an obstacle for JGB. Garcia stretches out every syllable in the Bushnell, and creates that hypnotic groove that defies time. As Garcia sings "Look around-round-round," a surreal feeling builds, as if the music is about to break on through to another dimension.

Like a moon-shot rocketing off the bat of Reggie Jackson, Garcia hits the "Prudence" solo out of sight from the get-go. It's out of character for Garcia, the master teaser, but he's overcome by emotion. America was reeling abroad and at home in the final leg of Jimmy Carter's fragile presidency, but as Jerry, John, Greg and Ozzie pour their hearts and souls into the final jam of the night, pure time out of mind ecstasy is achieved in the Bushnell. It's an aural assault, a steady barrage of guitar orgasm, and it's hard to fathom that this dynamic and symphonic sound is created by a quartet. For a little while, nobody is thinking about inflation, sitting in gas lines, or hostages in Iran.

A Garcia Band fan couldn't have expected anything more than what they received on 7-24-80. Better openers and encores than this "Sugaree" and "Dear Prudence" are few and far between. This Bushnell performance is a compilation of some of the most revered contemporary music ever created. Albums represented during this odyssey include: *Blood on the Tracks*, *White Album*, *American Beauty*, *The Harder They Come*, *Reflections*, and *Old & in the Way*. This performance seamlessly features many songs that would come to define the Jerry Garcia Band, and the consistency of the improvisation is stunning. The Grateful Dead and JGB are infamous for their performance valleys and peaks. There are no tens in this show, but all eleven songs would rate at a nine. Garcia loved these songs, and moving forward, his main objective was extending the jams within. For the Jerry Garcia Band, these were the days of awe and wonder.

10

BLUES FOR DIXIE

Deadheads exist to debate what was the Grateful Dead's finest year in concert. Most aficionados would identify one of the years from 1969 through 1977 as the band's heyday. My loyalties lie with 1972, and the powerhouse 1977 performances run a close second. As for rating the Garcia/Saunders years, which cover 1970 through 1975, and Reconstruction in 1979, I once again give the nod to 1972. By that time, Garcia, Saunders, and Kahn had a phenomenal band featuring a rich repertoire, and their growth probably exceeded any expectations that they had coming into the project. There's a free-flowing intensity to their playing; the music burns with innocence, a series of experiments yielding excellence. In the years to come, Garcia's musical endeavors outside of the Grateful Dead were all over the place. Between his involvement with Old & in the Way, and personnel changes in his lineup with Saunders, the purity of what they had in '72 was missing.

The night before the legendary Pacific High Studio show (2-6-72), Garcia and Saunders played Keystone Korner, a small San Francisco joint located on Vallejo Street. In a sixteen-month period that culminated on July 8, 1972, Garcia appeared on the Keystone Korner stage forty times with both Saunders, and the New Riders of Purple Sage. Guitar stalwarts Michael Bloomfield and Elvin Bishop headlined frequent jam sessions at the Keystone Korner during this era. Jazz pianist Todd Barkan bought the Keystone Korner in the summer of '72, and turned the place into a psychedelic jazz club featuring the likes of Miles Davis, Chet Baker, Bill Evans, and Dexter Gordon. Like many beloved clubs, this jazz haven was snuffed out in the eighties. Garcia Keystone Korner recordings are a rare commodity, but luckily there's 6-30-72, a well-circulated soundboard that features a slew of rare gems in all their coming-of-age glory.

Garcia starts the night with "It Ain't No Use," written by Jimmy Williams, Gary U.S. Bonds, and Don Hollinger, and first released on vinyl by Z.Z. Hill. I've listened to many versions of Garcia's "It Ain't No Use" through the years, and I was always under the misguided impression that it was a traditional blues tune accredited to somebody like Blind Willie McTell or Muddy Waters. Z.Z. Hill, a blues/soul singer from Texas, recorded an overproduced track of this song in 1971. Between the snickering intro rap and the superfluous horns, this song was bound for the scrapheap of insignificance until Garcia, or somebody else in the band, stumbled upon it. By stripping away the schmaltz, Garcia reclaimed the great blues core at the heart of "It Ain't No Use."

A smoky blues feeling permeates the club, courtesy of Garcia's howling guitar riff in the classic call and response motif. If you couldn't see the stage, one might have guessed that Buddy Guy or Albert King were on stage; that is, until Garcia's mournful, high-pitched vocal tones entered the equation. His voice releases pure heartache; there's no mock humor or anger: "I wanted you, but you wanted someone else. You ran away and left me, left me all by my, left me all by my, you left me all by myself."

I have an affinity for the second verse, which I've seen transcribed as: *There was a time/You was my pride and joy/The woman I loved/Like a child loves his toy.* I've always been under the impression Garcia sang, "Woman I love you, like a child loves his toy." That's the touch I like.

This tight rendition with Jerry's solos wrapping around Merl's swirling interlude concludes in eight minutes. "It Ain't No Use" appeared on *Live at Keystone* and *Compliments*. Through the years, this tune lingered in Garcia's live rotation, rarely overplayed, and always welcomed.

The fortunate Keystone Korner patrons must have been impressed by the next unrelenting jam, "Expressway To Your Heart." Putting things in historical perspective, this version doesn't come close to matching the epic perfection of the 2-6-72 "Expressway To Your Heart"; no version could tread on that holy turf. Luckily, those enjoying the show didn't suffer the burden of historical perspective; in fact, at least half of them probably couldn't identify the very instrumental they were tapping their feet to. Filling out the lineup with Saunders and Kahn, there's Bill Vitt on drums, and Credence Clearwater Revival's other Fogerty, Tom, on rhythm guitar. Make no mistake, this is a noteworthy jam. The band masterfully tinkers with volume and tempo—true jazz cats on the prowl. At one point, the jam dissolves into a murmur, and then Garcia turns it up and breaks it wide open—his axe spawns a tornado of sound. Being that it was rarely played, every "Expressway" is precious, and this just might be the second-best version. But I'll be damned, every time I hear this, I long for 2-6-72.

This gig was smack in the thick of historic times for the Grateful Dead, who had recently concluded their Europe '72 tour. The band followed with summer and fall tours that produced epic shows, such as 7-18-72 (Roosevelt Stadium), 8-27-72 (Kesey's Farm), and 9-21-72 (Philadelphia Spectrum). Down the line, some Grateful Dead originals would assimilate into the JGB rotation, but for now they just shared a cover here and there. "One Kind Favor," the third song on the Keystone Korner tape, was a number that the Dead had covered a few times in 1966. Written by the trailblazing bluesman Blind Lemon Jefferson, this was originally titled "See That My Grave is Kept Clean," and Jefferson's version is part of Harry Smith's *Anthology of American Folk Music*. A diverse array of musicians have covered this blues standard, including Bob Dylan on his eponymous debut album, and Garcia/Saunders would record "One Kind Favor" for *Live At Keystone*. Of all the versions I've sampled, 6-30-72 is the most satisfying.

As "One Kind Favor" takes shape, Garcia, Saunders, Kahn, Fogerty, and Vitt (sounds like a law firm, doesn't it?) slither into a Southern/Garcia groove, "House of the Rising Sun" meets "Mississippi Half-Step Uptown Toodeloo" on the California coast. Jerry's pipes unleash shrill howls that beg, plead, and scream for salvation. Prior to the chorus, Kahn thumps his bass like he's nailing a coffin shut with a power drill. The music's haunted with goblins, ghosts, and graves. Garcia's guitar's a-stinging—Cajun voodoo blues fortified by the demons that Saunders drains from the Hammond organ. Merl's got that grinding, swirling, gospel thing going, and on this night, it sounds as good as, or better than, it does at any other time during his stints with Garcia. These guys are in the moment, rowing the boat in unison. Jerry and Merl's partnership would roll on, yet, somehow, they could never recreate the passion they had in the summer of '72, when they were reckless, romantic warriors carrying on the traditions of Bourbon and Beale Streets, spreading the sounds of liberation to their peers.

Fogerty takes lead vocal on Fats Domino's "Sick and Tired," and the fun factor explodes. I can envision a young and reasonably fit Jerry in the jazz club. A contagious smile infiltrates his bushy black beard as he chimes in on harmony and bounces on the balls of his feet, and then his guitar does all the talking, "a- pickity-packety-pickity-packety- pickity-packety- pickity-packety- pickity-packety- pickity-packety- pickity-packety- pickity-packety- pickity-packety," in just about every variation of the boogie-woogie scale that he could muster.

Garcia continues to cultivate a Southern ambiance with an atmospheric performance of Jesse Winchester's "Biloxi." Aside from Dylan and Hunter, Winchester was, perhaps, Garcia's favorite contemporary lyricist. Oddly enough, Garcia didn't play any Winchester compositions after '76. It's a shame, because Garcia's soft, sophisticated arrangements suit Winchester's vivid imagery. Garcia has Keystone Korner under his spell and beneath Mississippi skies as he massages them with hushed tones: "The sun shines on Biloxi. The air is filled with vapors from the sea…We are splashing naked in the water. And the sky is red from off towards New Orleans." Guitar solo two slowly steams; the licks bubble and multiply. These Winchester songs, "That's a Touch I Like," "Every Word You Say," and "Biloxi" are the unheralded gems of Garcia's early oeuvre.

A torrid "That's All Right Mama" is followed by "The Night They Drove Old Dixie Down," that's paced somewhere in between The Band's brisk version, and the dawdling JGB versions to come. This completes a five-song segment rooted deep down in the land of Dixie. It's unlikely Garcia consciously prearranged this homage, although blessed accidents will occur if you have the wisdom and musical palate of Chez Garcia. The glitz of these '72 gigs is that there was no existing blueprint in place. JGB tours would go on to have diversified set lists, but like Grateful Dead tours, there was a protocol to the flow of the show—certain songs fit into certain slots. A band can't flourish in a continual state of chaos, no matter how talented they are. Eventually they settle into patterns and migrate south for the winter.

On June 30, 1972, Americans listening to AM radio were bidding farewell to Sammy Davis' "The Candy Man" as the number one song, and welcoming Neil Diamond's "Song Sung Blue," to the top of the heap. Those at the Keystone Korner were experiencing music that was lonesome and a million miles from home. With the sixth song of the night, the band put the pepper to Dylan's "It Takes a Lot to Laugh, It Takes a Train to Cry." Despite the fact that this song has landed in four of my top ten greatest Garcia performances, it wasn't a frequently played number. This 6-30-72 "Train" is full of vitality, a scorcher in every way. Garcia's euphoric vocal phrasing is filled with visceral outbursts and flourishes. It sounds as if he's granting the song the privilege to play him as it pleases. A smooth groove rolls, à la *Highway 61 Revisited*. Garcia yodels, "If I die on top of the hilllllll!" Kahn, Fogerty and Vitt pummel their instruments BAMM-BAMM-BAMM-BAMM-BAMM… BAMM-BAMM-BAMM-BAMM-BAMM. "If I don't make it you know my baby will…" BAMM-BAMM-BAMM-BAMM-BAMM… BAMM-BAMM-BAMM-BAMM-BAMM.

Garcia's the architect of three yearning solos; each one's more intense and committed than the one that preceded it, and the duration of each solo is scientifically divine. Garcia explodes into his last foray with a screeching tirade of desire. It's the type of sound I'd like to have filling my mind if I were diving off a cliff in Acapulco. With a definitive "It Takes a Lot To Laugh, It takes a Train to Cry" in the bank, it was time to cover just a little more ground.

The cozy Keystone Korner crowd hollers as one as they immediately identify the FM Clapton hit, "After Midnight," and it's a good thing they're happy, because Mr. Garcia would spend the next sixteen minutes fiddling around with JJ Cale's classic. The band repeats the same chord progression as Garcia shifts the aural landscape, navigating jazz, blues, and rock. This long instrumental lacks identity and purpose, but if one listens with patience, there's a lot of meat here—Garcia's phrasing vacillates from searing to sneaky as the band supports his every whim. Saunders excavates a lavish solo, and Vitt leads the charge when Garcia shifts from jazz riffs to rock and roll. Initially, this "After Midnight" didn't thrill me; it lacks the authority of future JGB versions. But it's an opportunity to hear Garcia chasing down the mojo.

Garcia transitions from shaman to public address announcer when he proclaims: "Hey, anybody here got a green Triumph, license plate number 6128ATO? Whoever's car it is you gotta go out and hassle with it. For some reason or another."

You gotta go out and hassle with it? It's clear Garcia isn't copasetic with announcements that interrupt his show. After the announcement hassle, there's a lengthy tuning break. Hopefully the patron with the car issues returned in time to hear "Money Honey," the rock 'em sock 'em bridge between "After Midnight" and the ensuing twenty-one minute blues mirage.

It begins slow and soft. "There's a last train to Jacksonville. I'm gonna get on it, baby, you know I will. Say you'll try, go ahead and try. To forget all the pain I've brought you," murmurs Jerry. Yes, it's another tearjerker, and the chord progression is reminiscent of the Grateful Dead's "Black-Throated Wind." "Are You Lonely For Me" is a hard-charging tune that was a number one R&B hit for Freddie Scott in 1967. In Garcia's world, these underappreciated three- and four-minute gems need to be celebrated; all the emotion that lies within must be expanded to be experienced. The first instrumental sets the tone—a lost and lonely journey that will resolve itself on Jerry's timetable. At the end of the second and final verse, Garcia howls, "I'm lonely baby, lonely and blue. I'm lonely baby, I'm a-lonely for you. Ah girl...Yes I am!"

The heavens have opened. Here come the blues, pouring down like hail. Garcia's men are coming through in waves, communicating in a unified, hypnotic trance. Garcia's improvising on a mound of sound, a skier riding the course, fantastically in and out of control. At times it's an amazing spectacle; there should be 100,000 people swaying and waving banners as they watch a closed-circuit broadcast of this in a soccer stadium. At times it's long-winded, but Garcia forges ahead. Take what you need and leave the rest. One wave of blues follows a funky groove, and then another wave of blues washes over that. Garcia breaks it down over and over again until "Are You Lonely For Me" crackles into freeform improvisation, Ornette Coleman territory. Todd Barkan was transforming Keystone Korner into San Francisco's psychedelic jazz treat, and this was Garcia's segue to a new era. The improv seems like it's running out of steam as the tape ends, but unsubstantiated reports claim that Garcia jammed for another hour and brought a guest guitarist on stage. It's certainly plausible.

There comes a time when the virtue of groundbreaking genius fades. Sure, Dylan gave us *Blood on the Tracks* a decade after *Highway 61 Revisited* and *Blonde on Blonde*, but it was a continuation of genius, not a quantum leap as stunning as what he had done from '61 to '66. In Garcia's kingdom, there would be no quantum leaps after 1972, just sustained genius for another decade or so. Sustained genius for ten years is nothing to sneeze at. The show from 6-30-72 is an unfettered glimpse into the soul of Garcia, a man who still had a deck full of aces at his command.

11

12-13-83 KEAN COLLEGE

JAZZ CATS ON THE BANDSTAND

If there's one venue that exemplifies the relative anonymity and abundant joys of the JGB experience in the early '80s, it has to be the Wilkins Theatre at Kean College (which has recently graduated to Kean University). With a fairly simple aerodynamic design, outrageous acoustics, and a seating capacity of 953, Wilkins Theatre was a Garcia-lover's dream destination. Located in Union, New Jersey, Kean College is seventeen miles from Manhattan, a half-hour drive in reasonable traffic conditions. With the Grateful Dead selling out multiple dates at the Philadelphia Spectrum and Madison Square Garden in 1983, these early and late shows at Kean College on 12-13-83 are the last of the Mohicans, the final time JGB will perform for an audience of less than one thousand paying customers in the Northeast. And believe it or not, on this wintery eve, tickets only cost fourteen dollars.

Garcia had already established a brief legacy at Kean College. On 2-28-80, the JGB quartet rocked an outstanding pair of shows in Wilkins Theatre that were recorded and released in 2004 as a triple CD titled, *After Midnight*. The stupendous recording features the striking three-headed beast, After Midnight > Eleanor Rigby > After Midnight, and Robert Hunter joined JGB for lively versions of "Tiger Rose" and "Promontory Rider." JGB also finished off a fall tour with a pair of rudimentary shows at Wilkins Theatre on 11-15-82. It must have been a gas for Garcia to play this pristine theatre, a short cab ride from Manhattan's bustling West Side—a secret oasis for the prudent Deadhead.

Those on hand for the early show on 12-13-83 witnessed a six-song set with an encore. There were fine performances of "Second That Emotion" and "Deal," but a JGB fanatic might ask, "Where's the beef, Jerry?" Playing two shows in one night was a bit of a challenge for Garcia, since he rarely repeated any songs. Let's say Garcia's near the end of his first show and the desire to play "Dear Prudence" strikes him. A wiser, less emotional voice in his head is likely to remind him that maybe he should save "Dear Prudence" for the late show. Conversely, when Garcia's in the thick of his late show, his options are diminished based upon what he played in the early show. That partially explains why neither an early nor late show has yet to make my historic performance list. However, the early/late show experience was a win-win for JGB and their flock. Garcia doubled his profit, and with the reasonable price of admission, most fans didn't mind paying and staying for a doubleheader. Any fans who saw the early show and didn't pony up for the late one on 12-13-83 made a tragic mistake.

Full-bodied marathon jams were ubiquitous for JGB in 1983. Another endearing quality of this year's shows was the reemergence of *Cats Under the Stars* selections in the rotation. Garcia kicks off the Kean late show with "Cats Under the Stars." I can't fathom why Garcia ditched this song in '78 after only playing it a few times. "Cats" was a gratifying addition to the short list of JGB openers. As the song begins, a funky groove juts ahead with an exuberant mix of sophistication and suspense, and the lyrics foreshadow the journey to come: *Cats on the blacktop, birdies in the treetop/ Someone plays guitar that sounds like a clarinet… Cats on the bandstand, give 'em each a big hand/Anyone who sweats like that must be all right…Time is a stripper doing it just for you.*

In Wilkins Theatre, Garcia's the stripper, stripping away time constraints just for you. Wave after wave, his guitar leads circle around the same chord progression, creating a hypnotic vortex that's pleasing to listen or dance to. There are no dramatic or stunning moments, just a gradual rise of intensity. The music's engaging, yet there's total comfort—the band and the audience are floating inside a warm womb; everything's groovy. Garcia sings the last line, "Cats down under the stars" repeatedly, and no matter how many times it's sung, you crave more—you didn't want to cut the umbilical cord.

This is the last show of a prodigious year for the JGB, and Garcia's cruising for kicks as he hops into "Catfish John." The Cats > Catfish combo is a small step for mankind, and a giant step for JGB—anything to break up the monotonous relationship of "How Sweet It Is" and "Catfish John." As Jaclyn LaBranch and Dee Dee Dickerson harmonize the opening chorus, Garcia can barely be heard. When he croons alone, Garcia's voice is ragged, haggard, and hollow. Throughout this fall tour, Garcia's voice lost the battle, night after night. Decades of relentless smoking and drug abuse had wreaked havoc on one of his greatest attributes. On the other hand, his guitar virtuosity showed few signs of decay during the tour. There were spots of sloppiness here and there, but for the most part, Jerry's jams were adventures of creative resolve. For the final JGB affair of the year, Garcia's in a spectacular place; inspiration pours from his Tiger guitar. It's a triumphant State of the Union address. In spite of all the touring wear and tear, and his unhealthy appearance, Garcia was still on a mission to thrill his loyalists, and on any given night, he was still the most gifted shaman on the planet.

Although I've never actually seen a catfish move through water, the sounds of Garcia's guitar mixed with the swampy texture of Melvin's organ imbue my mind with a glimpse into the plight of a catfish plowing through a muddy river. And as the Kean instrumental develops, the picture becomes clearer. This catfish is a plump stud, stronger and faster than other catfish; let's call him the Charles Barkley of the river. And there's no slowing down. Lo and behold, Garcia keeps turning over the melody, and with each round, the intensity and velocity escalates. Feeding off the buzz spreading through the crowd, the Bearded One channels mass energy and redistributes it stimulating sonic waves.

A roar ripples through the diminutive theater, praise for an enchanting solo. Merl starts doing his thing, but Garcia's hyped; his chord play seizes the moment. JGB fires up their reggae motif, which on this night is exceedingly jubilant—that good ol' percolating coffee sound. The jubilant sound now conjures up images of drunken revelers swerving and swaying in a conga line as their cruise ship closes in on the eastern shore of Puerto Rico under the watchful eye of a new blue moon. Seals and Garcia play off of each other wonderfully. It's delightful and fancy-free, as if Garcia's kissing all his troubles and woes goodbye. As he comes down the homestretch, the loudness of Garcia's guitar is jarring, like a pitchfork to the brain, as he shreds the crescendo to the screaming approval of his devotees. Going down that road of ranking versions, this "Catfish John" comes in at number two, just behind the massive Music Mountain "Catfish."

Clever song selection is a telltale sign of an immortal evening with JGB. That criteria is met, overwhelmingly, as Garcia follows Cats/Catfish with "Someday Baby," a number that had has been in exile for too long. Garcia's understated vocal timbre on this night suits "Someday Baby" just fine. To compensate for his thin vocals, when it's jam time, Garcia dials up guitar volume—Jerry's Kids are in heaven. It's an authoritative instrumental with a swiping Seals solo sandwiched between Garcia's mayhem—classic blues with splashes of gospel, cool jazz, and acid rock. Kahn and David Kemper lay down a pulsating, sturdy beat. Kemper, the reliable, consummate musician, joined JGB in the summer of '83, replacing Greg Errico on drums. This show's an instant classic. Garcia is a real huckleberry. After an inauspicious early show, he's suddenly pulling rabbits out of thin air.

"Love in the Afternoon," the second of four *Cats Under the Stars* numbers appearing in the late show, has a regal ambiance, despite Garcia's lyrical flubs. *Rhythm, wine, a touch of Jamaica/Twilight time with a Kingston lady* is the lyric that best describes the musical land-scape. JGB's evocative playing puts you right on the mystical Caribbean Island, where, a year earlier, the Grateful Dead played a show at the Bob Marley Performing Arts Center in Montego Bay. One of the distinctive highlights of this version is the ting-tung chime of Melvin's organ; it sounds as if he's playing a xylophone. Oh, the interplay between Kahn, Seals, and Garcia! The sonic waves are trippy, serene, and their effect is rejuvenating.

JGB whacks Kean College out of collective hypnosis with "Tangled Up in Blue," a barnburner to end the set. During the between-verse solos, Garcia's fingers wiggle up and down the fret board like dancing sausages. You can hear that restless-on-the-road attitude that complements Dylan's lyrics. During the tour de force finale, Kahn's throbbing bass goes off like a police siren, and Kemper's a percussion bully, applying all the pressure he can in that direct style of his. Revolution fills the air, and then suddenly, the propulsion eases; there are new paths to explore. The sound softens as Garcia noodles—there's a post-Miles Davis *Bitches Brew* kind of thing going on. This tinkering of tempo and volume was a new twist that JGB tried out on different numbers throughout the tour. This Kean "Tangled Up in Blue" isn't as bodacious as the 5-28-83 Cape Cod version, but it's a mighty fine variation.

By launching set two with "Rhapsody in Red," Garcia's intuitive sense of symmetry is on display again. Both sets commence with uplifting rockers from *Cats Under the Stars*, and set one and set two play out like side A and side B of an album. Each set, or side, is balanced by another number from *Cats Under the Stars*. I'm not implying that Garcia consciously planned this kind of thing out backstage, it's just that after juggling and shifting song rotations for so many years, he became a master composer who could asses any situation and prescribe the right melody. This skill also required the insight to know when *not* to play a song. Deadheads tend to be zealously loyal, but it's more than fanaticism that motivates them to collect hundreds and thousands of live recordings. Garcia was a problem solver, a savant who knew how to resolve musical riddles on the fly. A lot of today's jam bands go out there and "wing it," in hopes of finding that elusive Grateful Dead magic, but their efforts generally fail to produce a meaningful live canon. Essentially, whether the final product was subpar, sublime, or merely satisfactory, Garcia wove a distinctive album every time he took the stage—the shuffling of songs, and all the improvisation, seemingly had a logical progression all its own.

An intermission often changes the mood and flow of a show, but "Rhapsody in Red" picks up right where "Tangled Up in Blue" let off—unflinching music highlighted by raunchy rhythms and jazzy overtones. In the his final JGB performance of the year, Garcia blasts through to a new level of artistry through gritty determination and pure will. It's inspirational to hear his commitment in spite of his grave health issues at the time. Garcia's strange physical presence only made him appear more godlike. When the music was inexplicably brilliant, like it was on this night, Garcia seemed immortal, or heroic at the very least.

Side B slides along with "Gomorrah," Garcia's last *Cats Under the Stars* performance at Wilkins Theatre. After all the fire and brimstone jamming, a cautionary biblical tale fits like a glove. Garcia sings of ancient times as if he's conversing with Lot: "Who gave you your orders? Someone from the sky. I heard a voice inside my head, in the desert wind so dry." Jaclyn and Dee Dee chime in with spirited gospel vocals. For the time being, Kean College is a sacred seminary, and Wilkins Theatre is church. I hate to dampen the mood here, but I must confess that Garcia's voice struggles, and lyrics are butchered, but the band's crisp playing makes this an enjoyable listen.

Although there isn't much gas left in Garcia's tank, he drops the "Don't Let Go" stamp of immortality on 12-13-83. The song casts its euphoric spell on Kean College. As Garcia and mates head into the freeform jam, the sounds get stronger and stranger. It's a campaign against sanity—jazzy riffs echo and reverberate through the theatre, screeching strings are scratched and pinched this way and that way. This is the type of music that dwells in imaginary terrain, in the abandoned alleyways where jazz cats jam with Delta bluesmen. "Don't Let Go" swirls and crosses the line into the Grateful Dead weirdness of Mind Left Body Jams. Kahn loves these weird jazz adventures, and Seals is really stepping out; at times, Melvin charts the direction of the jam. At this juncture in his JGB tenure, Seals was a made member of the band, and as an untouchable, he was taking more chances without forsaking his role as the glue that held the groove together. Anyway, nothing could hold this "Don't Let Go" jam together. After ten minutes of probing, it's cosmically out of whack. On this tour, Garcia had established a precedent of not singing the final chorus on some of the songs, instead choosing to segue into a new song. Once "Don't Let Go" drifts too far from shore, the band pauses for a deep breath and charges into "Midnight Moonlight." There will be no encore. Garcia has given it his all.

The performance on 12-13-83 is stacked with many admirable attributes, both tangible and intangible. There's the intimacy of the Wilkins Theatre; an intimacy that would never be experienced again by Garcia fans on the East Coast. As a band, with David Kemper clearing the path, JGB jammed further and farther than anybody around, with the possible exception of the Grateful Dead. That's a compliment, because 1983 was one of the last banner years for the Grateful Dead. But above everything else, there was Garcia's miraculous effort. His body was a ticking time bomb—any little thing could trigger a serious medical situation. Yet, while he was still breathing, he could lift the spirits of others and continue to build a never-ending musical legacy, so he kept on keeping on, like a bird that flew.

12

2-5-81 LEHIGH

PRUDENCE TEARS

In the heart of the Lehigh Valley, in the city of Bethlehem, Pennsylvania, there stands Stabler Arena, a magnificent 6,000-seat venue on the campus of Lehigh University. Thanks to its crisp acoustics and intimate ambiance, Stabler Arena is a popular touring destination for bands in demand, and several music videos have been filmed there. In the wintertime of 1981, Bethlehem Steel, a mighty symbol of American industrial manufacturing leadership, was in dire straits. The following year they would report a loss of $1.5 billion dollars. With the closing of industrial factories in neighboring Allentown, the Lehigh Valley was becoming a ghost town for blue-collared workers. This region needed spiritual uplifting, and reasons to celebrate. Garcia's mission on 2-5-81 was to pick up his Tiger guitar and play the role of "Dear Mr. Fantasy." With the brilliant venue, rowdy East Coast fans, and the arcane history of the region, this was the type of gig Jerry coveted. Later in the year, Garcia would return to Stabler Arena on 9-25-81 for a show with the Grateful Dead.

Lehigh is the tenth show of the Melvin Seals era. At the Keystone Palo Alto, on 12-20-80, the duo of Seals and Jimmy Warren replaced

Ozzie Ahlers on keyboards, and Daoud Shaw replaced Greg Errico on drums. The Ahlers and Errico JGB quartet was operating on a masterful level, yet Garcia was still searching for that soulful R&B feel that he had in his early days with Saunders. Garcia's quest was satisfied when he recruited Seals, a San Francisco native who first performed gospel music in church, and went on to play with artists such as Chuck Berry, Charlie Daniels, and Elvin Bishop.

How sweet it is to hear JGB in the Motown groove again. The second set from Stabler Arena is where the band transcends; but the first set is way above average, even if the song selection isn't. Out of the standard "How Sweet It Is," "Catfish John," "That's What Love Will Make You Do" opening, "Catfish" is the catch of the day. Jerry enunciates the lyrics conscientiously, twisting each word to squeeze out maximum pleasure, much to the delight of the howling locals. The instrumental is edgy, and even though it's show number ten for these guys, they've already established that funky/reggae chord progression that would become their pride and joy. Seals' earthy organ tones are thick, and Warren's ring tone sounds play off that nicely. I've yet to stumble upon a critique that praises Warren's playing; in fact, most reviews trash his efforts, and some suggest he was in the band because he was some kind of drug courier. I'm not suggesting that we nominate Warren for the Rock and Roll Hall of Fame; in fact, I'm not going to vouch for his virtuosity. But his contributions complemented the JGB sound in a positive way.

The set ends with a Berry on Dylan sandwich— a sizzling "Let it Rock" is stacked in between "Simple Twist of Fate" and "Tangled Up in Blue." Out of the billowy, lazy haze of "Simple Twist of Fate," Garcia hammers a steel-driving tribute for the working men of Bethlehem. Daoud Shaw's drumming style jives with the sounds inside Garcia's mind; he's got that stoned, hypnotic beat thing going. Jerry jolts Stabler Arena with lightning guitar strikes, yet there's that all good things in all good time pace. Nothing's pressurized—everything resolves as it should.

The Lehigh tape is an outstanding audience recording. Of the shows I've written about, Lehigh only trails Music Mountain for the highest quality boot in *Positively Garcia*. The Stabler Arena is a haven for performing artists and bootleggers. The audience was East Coast rowdy, boisterous enough to rouse Jerry, but not as bombastic as the fanatics in Albany on 11-4-81. Give or take ten minutes, Bethlehem is an hour car ride from Philadelphia or New York City, so Stabler Arena draws a balanced blend of locals, city folk, and college kids.

Lehigh is loving JGB, and the boys in the band return their affection by christening set two with "Sugaree." Jerry's got the holy mojo rollin' as he slices away the outer layers of the "Sugaree" onion with his initial foray. I'd like to acknowledge Robert Hunter for penning such wonderful verses, but thanks to Garcia, in my mind, "Sugaree" is nothing more than a trilogy of thrilling solos. Solo two commences with tasty low notes that probe the bottom of the barrel. Garcia starts whipping things around pretty good as he ascends to mid-range scales. Garcia's on a Lehigh University stage, but it sounds as if he's performing for a select bumper crop of Juilliard students. This solo is an exhibition of technical skill. Garcia's determined to cram every guitar scale into this lecture, from low to high frequency, with increasing velocity. He triggers those piercing notes into a tirade on a frequency that I've never heard from Garcia before, and it's unique because Garcia races forth, yet there's no emotional overload. The craftsmanship is stunning, and Garcia is master of the guild. This solo has serious attitude and nasty bite.

Sometimes when Garcia nailed a dominant second solo, the third and final solo tended to be truncated and subdued. As a spectator witnessing a live "Sugaree," whether or not Jerry would go psycho on the last jam was a suspenseful moment—to be, or not to be. No matter how much glory was packed into jam two, I was always disappointed when he soft-shoed the last jam. Nobody could have faulted Garcia for taking the easy way out in Lehigh. As the final adventure eases down the road, it sounds like a cradle gently rocking; but Garcia has no plans on putting "Sugaree" to sleep. Another creation materializes, like a butterfly emerging from a cocoon. Garcia's guitar sings gracefully from the land where the pretty picking rolls. There's no dramatic fanfare. Garcia's just fluttering and flapping his wings, lingering in the glow that has enveloped Stabler Arena. It's hard to find a "Sugaree" that covers more ground than this one.

JGB stomps boldly into "Harder They Come," and it comes off like an Appalachian swing dance party sponsored by a Colombian cocaine cartel. Oh, Mama, the magic carpet ride arrives in the form of that wild Brazilian JGB motif. Students and mountain men howl side by side as Jerry slithers down one more greasy trail. Kudos to drummer Daoud Shaw, who's guiding the beat exactly the way Garcia likes it.

"Oh, the streets of Rome are filled with rubble. Ancient footprints are everywhere," sings Jerry to the masses of Bethlehem, the latest symbol of American industrial decay. "When I Paint My Masterpiece" is the third Dylan offering of the night, which only seems right—the musings of a poet from the once-great mining town of Hibbing, Minnesota, soothing the souls of those assembled in Bethlehem. Garcia's singing is smooth like a rhapsody, and his axe work blisters. The guitar phrasing is ornery, the kind of stuff that'll burn your brain out if you listen too closely.

Strange things started happening to "When I Paint My Masterpiece" in the summer of 1987. After touring and performing with Bob Dylan, the Grateful Dead began playing "Masterpiece," and lo and behold, Bob Weir was the lead singer. I'm sorry, but that's outrageous and in poor taste. To be fair, Weir did a nice job, and the audiences enjoyed the defiled "Masterpiece"; but sweet Jesus, this was Jerry's baby! I imagine that Garcia gave Weir the go-ahead to sing "Masterpiece," but the Grateful Dead's version was a bore compared to the JGB "Masterpiece"; even the guitar solos were tame. JGB didn't play "Masterpiece" much after Jerry's coma, but oh, how that song shined in its prime—and it was never overplayed. Jerry judiciously broke it out on all the right occasions, such as 2-5-81.

What would a JGB show in a haunted American town be without "The Night They Drove Old Dixie Down"? Now with Melvin in JGB, "Dixie" is back after a twenty-seven-month vacation, and it's better than ever. It's as if Garcia is presiding over some kind of mass wake, and his songs are like prayers healing the congregation. The way Garcia moans, "They should never have taken the very best," will make the tiny hairs on the back of your neck stand at attention. This isn't your garden variety rock concert, and the segue into the next song brings more sorrowful bliss.

For the second time, JGB performs The Night They Drove Old Dixie Down > Dear Prudence. The handoff is awesome, and with Lennon's murder only two months earlier, this combo now links the death of the Confederacy with the symbolic death of the Sixties. There's clearly conflicted emotion as Jerry sings "Dear Prudence." The joy of the words is undercut by the gaping, raw wound left by the unspeakable tragedy. It almost sounds as if Jerry's sobbing—a few tears might be sliding down his cheeks. The carefully constructed instrumental that follows stands in stark contrast to the boundless buoyancy that comes through during the "Prudence" jam from Bushnell on 7-24-80, although the music in Lehigh is no less compelling. Garcia channels all the heartache in the arena and his guitar cries "Prudence" tears. It's a public grieving, celebration, and tribute, all rolled into one. It's an amazing twist of fate that "Dear Prudence" found its way into Garcia's rotation as an occasional guest while Lennon was still alive. Now, it was blossoming into the ultimate Lennon tribute, and an essential JGB classic.

"Midnight Moonlight" comes shooting out of "Dear Prudence." Following the melancholy mood of the previous songs, "Midnight Moonlight" is a zany release; the whacky energy of the music is cartoonish. It would make a nice soundtrack for a black and white episode of *The Little Rascals* or *The Three Stooges*. Electric bluegrass saturates the air—it's the last jig of the Psychedelic Hillbilly Winter

Jamboree in the valley. Jerry bids farewell to the enlightened and exhausted revelers. It was a wondrous winter eve in the valley, and it was just another day's toil for the JGB. Onward and forward to the next hog-eyed town.

8-20-81 KEYSTONE
BERKELEY

LONESOME AND A LONG
WAY FROM HOME

In my quest to compile the greatest JGB shows, I profusely studied set lists to see if there were any promising shows that I hadn't heard during my thirty years of collecting and chronicling JGB boots. Mulling over endless set lists, I discovered two shows from the summer of '81 at the Keystone Berkeley, that I had to hear. Both shows featured "Tough Mama," "(I'm a) Road Runner," "The Way You Do The Things You Do," "Don't Let Go," and "Lonesome and a Long Way From Home"; torrid tunes which had not been played since the JGB days of Keith and Donna Godchaux. Garcia broke these gems out from hibernation on 7-26-81, and played them again on 8-20-81. Through the mysterious magic of the Internet, I located and downloaded these shows with a few simple keyboard taps.

The recording of 7-26-81 Keystone is a soundboard. Besides the addition of Essra Mohawk and Liz Stires on vocals, JGB featured the same personnel as they had when they pillaged Lehigh earlier in the year. Mr. Garcia had a truckload of good intentions when he took the Keystone stage, but the opening "The Way You Do The Things You Do" missed the mark. Oh well, tsk tsk. A flaccid "Catfish John" followed. This was not a good omen, since a sizzling "Catfish" is a barometer of a fabulous show. With the exception of an inviting "Lonesome and A Long Way From Home," the other performances ranged from sloppy to mediocre. Essra and Liz, who had joined the band at a show in Santa Cruz a month earlier, were still striving to fit in. Let's give Mr. Garcia an A for effort and a C- for execution.

My last shot at striking gold was an audience recording from the Keystone Berkeley on 8-20-81. Right away there's good news and bad news. Garcia opens with "Sugaree," but the recording is flawed. It sounds like the recording mic was attached to a garbage pail, and a bartender was tossing empty beer bottles into the pail, intermittently, at a rate of about seven bottles per ten minutes. However, I'll take a subpar recording of a great show over a soundboard of a lame show any day. Anyway, once Garcia starts shaking and baking in that first solo, it's clear that he's an inspired man. It's a glittery "Sugaree"; all solos bustle with West Coast hipness. It lacks the pressurized East Coast punch of the Lehigh version, but it's gorgeous in its own way: the velvety swipes of Melvin's organ, the aromatic *oom-pah* of Kahn's bass, and the electrified chimes of Garcia's strings.

Batting in the second spot is "I Second That Emotion," another tune that has recently reappeared in the rotation. Garcia had a thing for singing "well" before choruses, and this tune provided him ample opportunities. "Well, if you feel like loving me, if you got the notion, I second that emotion. Well, if you feel like giving me a lifetime of devotion, I second that emotion." Other favorites include: "Fire, fire on the mountain. WELL! Fire, fire on the mountain...Knock, knock, knocking on heaven's door. Well I'm, knock knock knockin' on heaven's door...Well, West L.A. Fadeaway...Well, you could have been anything that you wanted to, and I can tell the way you do the things you do." *Well, well, well, you can never tell*. Well, you get the idea. With the ladies providing harmony, and Melvin amply filling Saunders' shoes, Jerry was in Motown heaven. Every aspect of this tune is appealing.

"*Ka-ping-crash!*" Another beer bottle bites the dust as the next song begins. "Bing bang boom, bing bang boom…Love, in the afternoon, outside the window, an organ grinder's tune." The music's freaky as a flashback. Hippies are spinning and twirling in a time warp as if it's the Carousel Ballroom and the year is 1968.

The psychedelic dust of "Love in the Afternoon" is blasted away by a rambunctious "Tough Mama." Garcia scoots out of the gate; the pace is quicker than Dylan's original. More bottles clank and break; the crashing complements the raucous pulse of "Tough Mama" as if the bottle breaker is employed by JGB. The mood is lewd and lascivious. Garcia can barely spit the words out on time. This is a different animal from the Legion of Mary version—not as spectacular or as long as the 7-4-75 rendition—but it's a titillating rush that strips the audience of its collective breath. Garcia covets this song, as does Dylan, though neither messenger will play it often—it's a special tune, too hot to handle on an everyday basis.

After seven psychotic minutes of JGB heat, Garcia transitions to the snail-paced ballad "Mississippi Moon," a refreshing precursor to the set finale, "(I'm a) Road Runner." In addition to the clever song selection and placement, Garcia's on a relaxed roll, effortlessly connecting a varied mix of musical styles and tempos. The addition of the female vocalists empowered JGB to expand their repertoire, and on this night, Mohawk and Stires are confident contributors. Of the three new tunes that are returned to the lineup, "I Second That Emotion" and "(I'm A) Road Runner" would become welcomed additions to many future shows, while "Tough Mama" remained elusive, only being played twice in 1982, and five times in 1990.

Since I'm spitting out numbers again, dig this: The Keystone Berkeley opened in 1972 and closed in 1984, which conveniently correlates with the years covered in *Positively Garcia*. In various configurations, Garcia played the Keystone Berkeley 206 times, an obscene amount more than any other venue. This dingy beer and jam joint had a capacity of around 500 people, and it usually featured local bands—some on their way up, some on their way down. The Keystone was Jerry's itty-bitty Brokedown Palace, the room where the iconic *Live At Keystone* was born. Shows at the Keystone were rarely announced or promoted till the day of the show. This was Garcia's Garage, a place where he could just show up and play without being engulfed by adoring masses, a place where he could fly to the moon, or plummet like a high-powered AFC offense in the Super Bowl. In the Keystone on 7-26-81, JGB fumbled through a pair of sets. On 8-20-81 they ascended the mountain of immortality, like the early Roman kings.

Out of the dreamy dusk of a balmy Berkeley eve, set two softly starts with "Knockin' On Heaven's Door." It's way after midnight, and the band plays cautiously, as if they're juggling eggs. It's a most unassuming opener. It's as if they're saying, "Hey, dudes, we don't mean to disturb the tranquility of your inner peace, or to infringe upon your cosmic space, but we gotta get on with the show." I'm fond of the slow ballad here; it aligns with the schizoid frequency of the show. The Keystone crowd howls and sings along to the leisurely reggae interpretation of Dylan's iconic tune. Garcia evokes a sonic journey right to heaven's doorstep. Like most "Heaven's Door" instrumentals, this one suffers from repetitive laziness. Garcia puts together snaking guitar runs during the verse, but instead of expanding upon what was just done, the band hops into a reggae-light shuffle, and Garcia has to press reset for round two, and three, and four, and ah, five—the jam never takes off. This continuous pattern of gaining ground and giving it back is the equivalent of watching tennis players holding their serve. That being said, I like this version because it's a quirky selection as a set opener.

The Keystone is transformed from a dingy dive into a sea of sparkling sanguinity and righteous virtue as Garcia sings, "You got a smile so bright. You know that you could be a candle. I'm holding you so tight, you know that you could be a handle." "The Way You Do the Things You Do" is the feel-good number of the JGB rotation, with its amusing love-struck sentiments: *As pretty as you are, you know you could have been a flower/If good looks was a minute, you know that you could be an hour.*

Jerry, Essra and Liz harmonize a gorgeous tribute to The Temptations. Pangs of pleasure pour from Garcia's guitar—surging ecstasy celebrating a spiritual bond between Haight-Ashbury and Motown.

Once again, Garcia offers more evidence of his intuition for musical symmetry. Song number two from each set was a mid-'60s hit for Smokey Robinson, "I Second That Emotion," by Smokey Robinson and the Miracles, and "The Way You Do the Things You Do," by The Temptations. Further bolstering this notion of synchronicity is that, in 1969, "I Second That Emotion" was released as a single by Diana Ross and the Supremes, and The Temptations. The B side of that 45 is "The Way You Do the Things You Do." Seemingly random jolts of inspiration were often logical in Garcia's world.

The good times continue to roll with "Don't Let Go," a number that had been in hibernation for a couple of years. It's delightful to hear Jerry reuniting with an old flame. Keeping with the theme of the night, Garcia howls another "Well!" as two more bottles smash. There's a flirtatious temperament to the instrumental that's true to Roy Hamilton's 1958 hit. Instead of darting towards darkness, the band plows straight ahead with the snappy chord progression, and Garcia's hands are busy polishing the fret board—bright, liberating sounds cascade from the strings. The delirious crowd erupts as the snug, seven-minute jam concludes. Garcia's timing is succinct on this night.

Completing his trilogy of breakout songs from the 7-26-81 Keystone performance, Garcia serves up "Lonesome and a Long Way From Home," an essential JGB masterpiece that had its heyday during the Keith and Donna years. As the "Lonesome" journey begins, the tempo and chord structure is similar to "Tangled Up in Blue." Eric Clapton's compact version of "Lonesome and a Long Way From Home" from his eponymous solo album stoked Garcia's fancy. Co-written by Leon Russell, "Lonesome" spiritually captures the allure of the open highway, counterbalanced by the heartache of being far from the comforts of home—*something, something must be wrong...somebody help me.* Essra and Liz echo Jerry's pleas and Garcia testifies, "I-ah-I have never been so lonesome, and a long way from home." Jerry conveys the un-yielding American fascination with living on the road, and the flip side of that excess wanderlust—the pain of lingering loneliness and solitude.

Jerry's voice slowly yearns and burns, but the music is exhilarating, striking out with the infinite possibilities of a life-altering road experience. As the jam unfolds, the thrills multiply. Melvin's organ creates the scenery; Kahn and Shaw are operating in the fast lane; and Garcia brings the heat—layers of rippling rock and roll. This instrumental isn't as expansive as the versions from 1978, but it achieves its purpose within the flow of the show. It's the crowning moment of a triumphant night. However, this would be the last performance of "Lonesome and a Long Way From Home" for eight years. JGB played it five more times in 1989. Fortuitously, I witnessed one of these performances in Hartford on 9-5-89.

Those who were fortunate enough to be on hand for this Keystone gig were treated to an epic and unprecedented "Lonesome and a Long way From Home > Dear Prudence > Tangled Up in Blue finale—Clapton > Lennon > Dylan. "Dear Prudence" is buoyant, true to the bright tone of the show. With Melvin's rich organ sound, and Essra and Liz echoing Jerry on the "Look around round round" chorus, "Prudence" takes on a trippy, thicker sound, reminiscent of something from the *Magical*

Mystery Tour. There's a lot of color, texture, and substance to the big jam, but there's no almighty climax—the juicy quintessential West Coast JGB sound.

"Tangled Up in Blue" is better than ever before. The ladies strike up a "Tangled up in blue, yeah!" chant at the end of each pass during the first two solos. It's a touch I like. I can picture them out on stage in red and yellow USC cheerleader outfits rallying Garcia: "Tangled up in blue, yeah! Tangled up in blue." Garcia extends and shreds the final movement of the night. It's an all-out assault, a downhill skier accelerating from fast to warped speeds. "Tangled Up in Blue" is graduating from a beloved Dylan cover to an epic jam packed with a bright lights and big-city sound. Garcia's first, and only spoken words to the Keystone faithful are:

"Thanks a lot, see ya later."

These were blessed times for the Jerry Garcia Band.

Garcia picking away at the Keystone Berkeley, 8-20-81. ©Bob Minkin

13

KEYSTONE YEARS
ANTHOLOGY

In Harry Smith's *Anthology of American Folk Music*, there exists a world of music that's almost a genre unto itself. Greil Marcus refers to that realm as the Old Weird America. If an archivist such as Harry Smith can assemble a collection of folk tunes that speak of an Old Weird America, then an artist like Jerry Garcia should be able to enlighten us to a wilder and weirder America that's bound to cover just a little more ground. From 1972 through 1984, Garcia's live canon with his own bands produced an alchemist's brew of music that links Jimmy Rodgers and Blind Lemon Jefferson to the likes Bob Dylan, Robert Hunter, and Jessie Winchester on a psychedelic playing field that erases the boundaries between past, present, and future—time out of mind transcendence. Garcia's sophisticated style also blurs the lines between jazz, rock, blues, gospel, reggae and bluegrass. The common bond of Garcia's music from these years is the ever-evolving American experience. It's impossible for an artist to create a work that comes close to capturing such a vast enterprise, but Garcia does a phenomenal job of reflecting that experience.

Since the life of the Keystone Berkeley (1972-1984) corresponds with the years of *Positively Garcia*, and Jerry played there 206 times,

I'll refer to my Garcia compilation as the *Keystone Years Anthology*. To mirror what Harry Smith did with his anthology, I've set up six categories to group the songs that Garcia played. Each grouping consists of performances discussed in this book, and each grouping fills up a side of a CD in a hypothetical box set.

Side one is all Dylan. It's not a JGB show without a serving of Hibbing. Side one is a luscious loop, beginning and ending with different versions of "It Takes a Lot to Laugh, It Takes a Train to Cry." There's a whole lot of jamming here. Garcia was as generous with his improvisation as Dylan was with his words. These tunes dream, scheme, burn and yearn—visions of hope under the microscope. "The Wicked Messenger" and "Going, Going, Gone" are two fabulous Dylan covers from this period not represented here, simply because they weren't in any of the performances I discussed. In later years, Garcia would expand his Dylan repertoire with "Forever Young," "I Shall Be Released," and "Señor (Tales of Yankee Power)." If Jerry would have lived longer, he surely would have had a kick covering Dylan's newer stuff. It would have been pretty cool to hear him play "Trying to Get to Heaven," "Mississippi," or "Nettie Moore."

Dylan wasn't Garcia's partner in collaboration, but Jerry had the next best thing. Side two of the *Keystone Years Anthology* celebrates San Francisco's bard extraordinaire, Robert Hunter. These chosen performances stand on their own as a testament to the diversity of Garcia's virtuosity. The first four numbers are acoustic classics performed at the Oregon State Penitentiary in Salem. Garcia cuts loose on the remaining five electric numbers, bringing Hunter's inspirational sketches to life. These offerings are hypnotic, and robust, displaying the many shades of Garcia's soul.

Within this anthology, several songs could have ended up in different categories. For instance, on side three I opted to put Hunter's "They Love Each Other" with the other love ballads. I hear this grouping of songs as an ode to women, music, and living the life you love. Even though there are two slower ballads here, "Mississippi Moon" and "Love in the Afternoon," the sanguinity of Garcia's art is consistent. There are few complexities in the message; these tunes channel joyful experiences for the performers and the audience.

Garcia once said, "For me, I think the only danger is being too much in love with guitar playing. The music is the most important thing, and the guitar is only the instrument." On side four, Epic Jams, we'll embrace and relish the danger of Garcia being too much in love with guitar playing. The jams are everything—the songs are just vehicles. These instrumentals are so immense that they take on a life of their own, forming a new entity that swallows the original song, yet somehow, a melody line or a chord progression remains to tie it all together. These jams are extravagant, and logical in Garcia's own sweet way.

And then there's side five, Influences, the songs from Garcia's youth that left an indelible impression upon him; the songs that he couldn't shake, the songs that he had to glorify through expansion. These tunes are the embodiment of the bluesmen and first-generation rockers that Garcia loved—Ray Charles, Elvis Presley, Hank Ballard, Chuck Berry. As much as Garcia put his special spin on these performances, you can hear that his admiration for the original is as great as when he was first bitten by the song.

Since Garcia's recording career with the Grateful Dead began in 1967, I've used this year as the demarcation point for the songs compiled on side six, Inspirations. Although these are compositions from contemporary peers, there's an old-timey feel to them; a timeless wisdom lies within their core. This is contemporary Americana, forever propagated by San Francisco's native son, Jerry Garcia. For the purposes of Inspirations, I grant Jimmy Cliff US citizenship.

There you have it—liner notes to my hypothetical box set, the *Keystone Years Anthology*. As of the publication of *Positively Garcia*, none of these performances have been officially released, although there are a good number of Deadheads who have all these shows in their collection. Happy hunting.

DYLAN
It Takes a Lot to Laugh, It Takes a Train to Cry 2-6-72
When I Paint My Masterpiece 2-5-81
Positively 4th Street 2-17-80
Tough Mama 7-4-75
Simple Twist of Fate 7-24-80
Tangled Up in Blue 5-28-83
It Takes a Lot to Laugh, it Takes a Train To Cry 6-30-72

HUNTER
Friend of the Devil 5-5-82
Run for the Roses 5-5-82
Ripple 5-5-82
Reuben & Cerise 5-5-82
Cats Under the Stars 12-13-83
Sugaree 2-5-81
Mission in the Rain 11-4-81
Rhapsody in Red 5-31-83
Deal 11-4-81

LOVE BALLADS
How Sweet It Is 6-16-82
That's a Touch I Like 2-6-72
They Love Each Other 5-31-83
Mississippi Moon 5-31-83
The Way You Do the Things You Do 8-20-81
I Second That Emotion 8-20-81
Love in the Afternoon 6-16-82
That's What Love Will Make You Do 5-31-83

EPIC JAMS
Expressway To Your Heart 2-6-72
Don't Let Go 5-28-83
Dear Prudence 5-28-83
I Was Made to Love Her 2-6-72
After Midnight > Eleanor Rigby > After Midnight 2-17-80

INFLUENCES
Mystery Train 7-24-80
(I'm a) Road Runner 11-4-81
Money Honey 2-17-80
That's All Right Mama 2-6-72
Tore Up Over You 7-4-75
Lonely Avenue 2-6-72
Let it Rock 6-16-82

INSPIRATIONS
I'll Take a Melody 7-24-80
The Harder They Come 5-31-83
Catfish John 6-16-82
It's No Use 6-30-72
The Night They Drove Old Dixie Down 6-16-82
Lonesome and a Long Way From Home 8-20-81
Midnight Moonlight 5-28-83

REFLECTIONS OF THE JGB

How sweet it is. Garcia at Music Mountain, 6-16-82. ©Bob Minkin

14

MISSION IN PASSAIC

An unspeakable tragedy...resisting the irresistible...
Grateful breakthroughs and revelations...dazed
and confused in Passaic...Van Halen flashbacks...
paranoia and euphoria in the Palladium...

By the time I staggered into the Capitol Theatre in Passaic, New Jersey on November 6, 1981 for my first Jerry Garcia Band show, I was a Jerry Junkie. My ascent into full-blown Garcia obsession was fast and furious. It's odd, because when the year began, I couldn't fathom why anyone would follow the Grateful Dead, and the JGB was a complete mystery to me.

I'd just turned seventeen when John Lennon was murdered outside the Dakota. It was December 8, 1980, and I was watching the Miami Dolphins and New England Patriots on Monday Night Football when Howard Cosell went from announcer of a trivial contest to the man who had the awful burden of having to inform a national TV audience that this was the day that the music had died again, except this time, it wasn't a plane crash.

Remember, this is just a football game, no matter who wins or loses. An unspeakable tragedy confirmed to us by ABC News in New York City. John Lennon, outside of his apartment building on the West Side of New York City. The most famous of perhaps all the Beatles, was shot twice in the back and rushed to Roosevelt Hospital. Dead on arrival. Hard to go back to the game after that news flash.

It was hard for anybody to go back to anything after that news flash. I was a high school dropout, passing time by working part-time on a General Equivalency Diploma at Rockland Community College. My entire life had been consumed by music, and I was already growing nostalgic for the good old days of rock and roll. The latest releases by the Rolling Stones, Dire Straits and Van Halen paled in comparison to the ones that preceded them. Paul McCartney was pumping out pop slop, and Dylan was a born-again Christian, the property of Jesus. Even the Grateful Dead, who I only knew through *Skeletons in the Closet* and *American Beauty*, had gone disco with *Shakedown Street*, and they looked like a bunch of old fairies on the cover of *Go To Heaven*. Hendrix, Morrison, Joplin, Allman, Croce, half of Lynyrd Skynyrd...dead, visionaries tragically cut down in their prime. With punk, new wave, and heavy metal on the rise, I was seeking fresh inspiration, but there was little, if anything, appealing on the horizon.

My dear friend and most trusted musical confidante, Doug Scmell, had recently become a Deadhead after a summer of sleep-away camp, but I couldn't grasp the Gospel of Garcia. The Grateful Dead name and skeletal imagery was cool, but Garcia didn't look like, or more importantly play like, a guitar god. Doug turned me on to a few Dead boots, but digging Garcia is an acquired taste. It's a different opiate from what was dished out on FM radio. We had an old-fashioned Mexican standoff. My buddy's predilection and allegiance for Garcia was baffling, and he was equally miffed by my resistance to the irresistible.

I was in the basement of my parents' house on a brown plaid sofa when Lennon was gunned down, and I was in the backseat of a tiny white Honda Civic when I was initially blown away by the Grateful Dead. On January 24, 1981, I went to the Nassau Coliseum and witnessed hockey history as Michael Bossy scored two goals in the last five minutes of an Islanders victory to become the second player in NHL history to score fifty goals in the first fifty games of the season. Being that Bossy was my favorite player, this was an absurdly thrilling spectacle. On the way home, my scraggly Deadhead acquaintance, Seymour, sparked a bone and popped *Europe '72* into the tape deck, and turned it up LOUD! And on this night it rang the bell in my brain. *Gotta get down to the Cumberland mine with Jack Straw from Wichita, because Mr. Charlie told me so.* Wow! I'd never heard anything like that—mysterious American tales from another time and place, played in an elusive and strangely sophisticated style. I knew I could find Grateful Dead records in the rock and roll section of my local record shop, Tapesville U.S.A., but these guys were so much more: folk, blues, jazz, bluegrass, R&B, and just about everything in between—an arcane brew of originals and covers tossed into a blender and served in the band's secret psychedelic sauce. If there was one tune that knocked me out of my head on that first listen, it was "Ramble on Rose." Jerry's lilting voice channeled Hunter's evocative lyrics, and the concise guitar solo reinforced that Jerry was indeed the leader of the band, whether he approved of that designation or not.

Six weeks after embracing the Grateful Dead, I saw my first show at Madison Square Garden, on 3-9-81. I waltzed into "The World's Most Famous Arena" during the exotic jam of "Feel Like a Stranger," and grabbed my seat up near the rafters. Garcia rewarded my presence by ripping through a sensational "Ramble on Rose," the song that I desired, early in the first set. However, I was still a neophyte when it came to appreciating live Dead. The lengthy jams weaving in and out and all around were hard to follow, especially the meandering between "Estimated Prophet" and "Uncle John's Band." I was observing one of the great concerts of 1981, although I was in the dark for most of it. I was of the mindset that live music should resemble the music I'd come to love on the albums. In order to dig the Dead, I had to change my way of thinking.

Soon after the MSG gig, I scored my first Grateful Dead bootleg, a ninety-minute BASF cassette tape of various performances from the band's legendary 1977 concert at Raceway Park in Englishtown, New Jersey. The free-flowing guitar odysseys of "Mississippi Half-Step Uptown Toodeloo" and "Eyes of the World" unclogged my mind to Garcia's silky-smooth and garrulous phrasing—he was circling the moon while other rock guitarists were motoring down the highway.

Collecting bootleg tapes became an immediate obsession. If I found out somebody had a live Dead collection, I'd scheme a way to get into their bedroom to inspect the precious cargo. I'd borrow and record anything I didn't have, taping quality be damned. For within any of these collections, there were masterpieces waiting to be discovered. These tapes had unlimited potential, and in my mind, any show could suddenly loom larger than iconic albums such as *Dark Side of the Moon*, *Abbey Road*, or *Who's Next*. The hunt for the next great Garcia jam was all-consuming; in fact, I indefinitely suspended listening to anything else. I quickly cultivated a killer stash of Dead boots: 2-14-70 Fillmore East, 12-5-71 Felt Forum, 7-18-72 Roosevelt Stadium, 11-4-73 Pauley Pavilion, 6-18-74 Louisville, 10-15-76 Shrine Auditorium, 5-8-77 Cornell, 7-8-78 Red Rocks. And with the Grateful Dead and Jerry Garcia Band on a never-ending tour, there was no foreseeable end to the boot pipeline.

My dreams were riding tall when Barry Ludes and I were rolling towards Passaic in his tan Pontiac Thunderbird on 11-6-81. Barry was a cat I used to hang with back in high school. He was lukewarm when it came to the Grateful Dead, but he had reliable wheels, a bag of skunk, and a small black vial of Quaaludes (hence the nickname). We each popped what I thought was a Rorer 714 on the way. By time we arrived in Passaic, those white, nickel-shaped tablets struck us like elephant tranquilizers. My memories from this evening at the Capitol Theatre are vague. A potent Quaalude can make you forget your name. From the early show, I recall the mellow yet evocative "plinkity-plinkity-plank" of Garcia's guitar during "Mississippi Moon," and a voracious "Deal" to end the set. Barry snored through the show as I stumbled, swaggered and swayed to JGB. When the jamming subsided, Barry snapped out of his slumber and slurred, "Howie, dude. I, ah, can't, ah, stay. Let's get out of here."

I was going nowhere. I patted Barry on the back and wished him well. You might wonder which was the more dangerous option: taking a death cruise with a teen nodding out from the effects of a killer Quaalude, or staggering around a rancid, crime-ridden New Jersey city by myself without a ride home. But on that night my mind was in no condition to debate the pros and cons of anything. I was on a mission, and missing the late show wasn't an option. Promoter John Scherr's Capitol Theatre was a renowned rock and roll joint, a prominent stop-off for any hot touring band. For Garcia, the Capitol Theatre was the Keystone East. In the four years prior to my first JGB show, Garcia had played in this 3,200-seat venue twenty times—ten shows with the Grateful Dead, and ten shows with the JGB. As I roamed the mean streets of Passaic between shows, I was fearless, as well as clueless, to the perils of my environment. I hoped I'd swerve into a familiar face, and if that didn't work out, well, there was no Plan B.

Perry, a former high school acquaintance, and the lead guitarist of a scrappy Dead cover band called the Roadrunners, found me staggering around the Capitol. Accompanied by Dave, the bulky redheaded drummer of the Roadrunners, we headed back to Perry's Buick Skylark to slam a few eight-ounce Miller Lite nips.

By the grace of Garcia, I bumped into the only cats I knew in Passaic. We split up inside the theatre. Perry and Dave found their seats and I found mine, I think. My remembrance of the late show would have been completely eviscerated by that filthy Quaalude if it were not for Jerry playing the tune I longed to hear, "Mission in the Rain." When Jerry dipped into that slow, salacious vocal prelude, I was twenty rows from the stage, smoking a Marlboro, and yodeling to the heavens with all my might. It was obvious that me and Jerry had something going on here. Whatever song I desired, my captain would play, and he'd play it better than he ever had before, just as he had done with "Ramble on Rose" at my first show. It took me seven years to track down a boot of this late show, and my hazy delusions of grandeur were confirmed. This is a monster "Mission in the Rain," right up there with the 11-4-81 Albany version two days earlier, on my eighteenth birthday. I must have been near the guy who taped this Passaic show, because I unmistakably hear my hysterical voice howling throughout Garcia's wicked solos:

"WOO-WHO-WHOO...YEEEEE-HEE-HEE, YAYA-YO! A-WHO-WHO-YEE, AHRRRRR...YEP-YEP-YEP, YEAH HAH!...GARCIA IS GOD!...YIPPEE YIPPIE YEAH YAHOOOOO!"

Four days after my mission in Passaic, I returned for more JGB at the Palladium, located in the gut of downtown Manhattan. The Grateful Dead had played a string of shows there in 1972, when the place was known as the Academy of Music. My only previous Palladium appearance was when I saw Van Halen there in the fifth row in 1979, a few weeks after they released *Van Halen II*. At the time, I believed that Van Halen were the Chosen Ones from my generation, the band that would go on to equal or surpass the Beatles and Rolling Stones in stature. Van Halen's first two albums fueled my adolescent fire—the unbelievable guitar feats of Eddie Van Halen, the surging sexuality in the high-pitched screams of David Lee Roth, the truculence of their macho sound. Their music made me feel like a conquering hero, and just in case that wasn't enough, I popped a couple of yellow jackets before the gig. Striding towards my fifth-row seat, I was revved up like Lawrence Taylor moments before a quarterback blitz. When the lights were dimmed, David Lee Roth stormed the stage with an assortment of flying mid-air splits in his candy-striped pants. Eddie's chords thundered as he struck guitar hero poses, and Michael Anthony pirouetted round and round with his bass. It was an incredible release; Van Halen played every song that my derelict friends and I expected to hear. My friend's father drove us to the Palladium, and my father picked us up. Oh, to be young again!

My musical tastes were refined and focused when I returned to the Palladium for JGB on 11-10-81. I'd cut my ties to the gluttony of progressive and hard rock acts that dominated FM airwaves. I only had ears for Garcia. I don't know how I arrived at the Palladium that night. I do recall dropping blotter acid onto my tongue in Union Square Park with Bob, a fellow Garcia devotee from my hometown. Walking into the Palladium was a vastly different experience from shuffling into the cozy, but prosaic Capitol Theater. As I hiked up the stairway to my balcony seat, I felt like royalty ascending inside one of the magnificent shrines of New York City. The regal interior was red and gold, and those colors started melting before my eyes. The air reeked of marijuana-laced excitement. I was a big boy experiencing high culture in the Big City, until the initial waves of acid began to strip away my sanity, leaving me as helpless as a poor man's child.

Garcia sailed through "How Sweet It Is" and "Catfish John" as I tried to settle into my acid trip. Garcia was up there doing his thing, and the acid was doing its thing, twisting my perceptions. I had a heightened sense of alertness to everything; the Marlboro smoke filling my lungs, the glowing of the ceiling, the warm blood surging through my veins, the strangeness of the musical vibrations entering my ears and surrounding my body, and a voice in my head telling me that there was no reversing course—I'd swallowed the paper on my tongue, and now I'd take the ride.

Garcia played "Sittin' Here in Limbo," a tune I didn't wish to hear, and a tune I wasn't sure I could endure. I wasn't familiar with Jimmy Cliff or JGB's snail-paced cover. A feeling of total unease gripped my mind, and my circulatory system was pumping, thumping, and jumping as time stood still. And Garcia was just standing there, catnapping on stage. Just when the end seemed near, Kahn began a spine-tingling bass solo in slow-mo. This superfluous drivel was sure to drive me insane.

Following a brief eternity, Garcia came to the rescue by bolting into "(I'm a) Road Runner," which reprogrammed my brain like a jolt of electroshock therapy. Garcia's guitar was a lightning rod, channeling and redistributing energy. The licks came fast and furious, tangerine and crimson, sweet and sour. The Palladium was sealed in a warm, embryonic glow. The magnetic heat pulsating from the band could tear the balcony from the rafters, but I was digging the magic carpet ride. I took a moment to glance at Bob. The pupils of his eyes were on fire. With a red bandana wrapped around his orange hair, and that cocky smirk of his, Bob looked like Captain Morgan on the tail end of a three-day bender. We were peaking and speechless, amazed by the multi-dimensional power of Garcia's friendly voodoo. As the rapturous jam peaked, a euphoric New York City roar engulfed the theatre.

What a glorious ordeal that was! Garcia forged ahead with "Simple Twist of Fate," a dastardly dirge, kryptonite for my peaking head. It hit me like a freight train of paranoia. Trapped in a velvety seat, torrents of adrenaline flashed through my body. This came off like a cross between "Sittin' Here in Limbo," and Chinese water torture. Kahn thumped another bass solo as a lighted nicotine stick dangled from his lips. Seconds seemed like minutes. Minutes seemed like days. In my overly exhilarated state, I didn't have the wherewithal to leave my seat to clear my head in the hall. I had no choice but to wait out "Simple Twist of Fate."

An outrageous, piercing guitar strike lifted me out of my seat and ignited "That's What Love Will Make You Do." From painstakingly mundane marathons to orgasmic thrills, I was Silly Putty® in Garcia's hands. Once again, I was experiencing Garcia's incendiary tone in a new way. I perceived extra dimensions within the jam; it was as if I was riding it on a surfboard, and the warm vibrations of the music balanced me. The set closed with "Deal," and finally I felt relief. I'd survived the demons within my mind, and now there was nothing left to do but smile, smile, smile. I embraced "Deal" with a spirited soft-shoe shuffle. The early show was over. Jerry said, "Thanks. See ya all later."

Fantastic. Bob and I gleefully bolted from our seats and scampered down the carpeted steps, which seemingly disappeared beneath my sneakers. As we touched down on the lobby floor, a sonic outburst filled the Palladium. That crowd roar could only mean one thing—JGB was coming back for more, and my darling, the opening licks indicated "Sugaree." Bob and I dashed back up those stairs as if we were trying to pass Jesse Owens in the 1936 Berlin Olympics. Back in the balcony, I tackled my 220-pound pirate comrade and yelled, "Jerry is God!" The phrasing of the "Sugaree" solos were demonstrative and crystal clear. It was a dramatic ending to a most intense affair.

Between shows, Bob and I met up with a pair of striking young ladies, goddesses we somehow knew from Spring Valley, a pair of high school seniors that were hip to the whole Grateful Dead scene. I'd first met these girls partying near the railroad tracks behind the Nanuet Mall, a gathering place for shoppers and teenage stoners. Laurie was a natural brunette hippie with floppy, robust breasts, and Tracy was a dirty-blonde-haired angel, a fox in tight jeans, with all the right curves in all the right places. We met them in front of the Palladium, and they waltzed into our night as memorable as any of Jerry's jams. I wistfully look back on that part of my night. If I knew then what I know now, and could do it all over again, I would have ditched Bob and Jerry at the Palladium and masterminded a ménage à trois with Laurie and Tracy. But since we were heading inside for the late show, our lovely dates used their God-given assets to whisk us past dumfounded ushers until we landed unoccupied seats with only seven rows of separation from JGB.

The atmosphere of shows couldn't have been more diverse. In the early show, Garcia dealt blazing fastballs and tantalizing changeups. In the late show, he scuffed the ball up and utilized a master's arsenal: curves, sliders, splitters, spitters and knuckleballs. "The Way You Do the Things You Do," was the uplifting opener for the late show. Jerry's girls harmonized as my girls sandwiched me in dance. The comfortable Motown opener was a welcome contrast to the extreme rollercoaster ride of the early show. Two years earlier, I was shuffling in just about the same spot, rocking with Van Halen and my hoodlum acquaintances. In that time and place, it would have been impossible for me to believe that I'd be dancing to R&B covers as interpreted by the immobile lead guitarist of the Grateful Dead.

"The Way You Do the Things You Do" featured a sparkling guitar solo, making it a classic performance along with "(I'm a) Road Runner" and "That's What Love Will Make You Do" from the early show. A few joints were passed around and, oh, mama, I began experiencing those acid paranoid blues again, especially when the lights were turned on for intermission after four songs. During the second set I was jazzed to catch my first versions of "Don't Let Go" and "Dear Prudence." It had been almost a year since the unspeakable tragedy of Lennon's murder, and JGB was helping heal the bleeding wound in the heart of this town, filling up the Palladium with hope and positive vibes. Although the jams in the second set were merely pedestrian, Garcia delivered exactly what I needed—a smooth ride.

These nights in Passaic and Manhattan affirmed and intensified my fascination with Garcia's music, although I must admit the power of these shows was an epiphany. I only had, maybe, a half-dozen JGB tapes, and I was still in the early stages of getting familiar with, and romancing their repertoire. I found these JGB shows more satisfying than my first two Grateful Dead shows at the Nassau Coliseum and Madison Square Garden. The intimacy of the venues had a lot to do with that, and the business-like aspect of JGB shows appealed to me. I would develop an appreciation for all the weird wonders of following the Grateful Dead: the colossal road trips, the ragtag army of devoted freaks, partying all day and jamming all night, and being part of an impromptu community and brotherhood. But alas, what I was really searching for was Garcia's next transcendent jam. The Grateful Dead's journey was a long strange trip, yet there was nothing clownish about JGB. This was just business, and I took it very personally.

15

A MAGNIFICENT OBSESSION

The golden road to unlimited devotion...miraculous
tales from the fast lane...Garcia's propaganda minister...
Deadheads swarm Music Mountain...Why is JGB playing in
a dump like this?...acid paranoid blues in the Felt Forum...

By the time I was on my way to Music Mountain for my first JGB rendezvous of the year, the humdrum status quo of my existence was shattered during the Grateful Dead's East Coast spring tour, most significantly, on 4-6-82 in the Philadelphia Spectrum. It was my first road trip, anywhere, for any reason. And it just so happened that an unfathomable April blizzard blanketed my hometown of Nanuet with eighteen inches of snow. However, that didn't deter my friends and me from embarking on a potentially perilous pilgrimage to the City of Brotherly Love.

A miraculous sonic expedition unfolded inside the Philly Spectrum. When The Boys saddled up their instruments for the second set, I craved four tunes: "Morning Dew," "Terrapin Station," "Sugar Magnolia," and "Shakedown Street." I felt clairvoyant, as if my wild mind could actually influence the Grateful Dead. Statistically, of the songs I craved, "Morning Dew" was the least probable, being that the Grateful Dead had only performed it twenty-one times in the last seven years. After the drum solo, the band briskly smoked a Truckin' > Other One combo, and I used all of my telepathic powers to sway Garcia towards "Morning Dew." A fractioned second of suspenseful silence followed "The Other One," and then Garcia struck the Holy Chord announcing "The Dew." Pure pandemonium broke loose in Philly! I grabbed my friend Scott by the waist and hoisted him into the air and proudly displayed him as if he was Lord Stanley's Cup. A young lady in front of me unleashed a steady succession of orgasmic screams; I still get chills when I think about the primal passion unleashed by that woman, and the collective emotional release from the crowd. The Great Garcia had pleased me with "Ramble on Rose" at MSG, "Mission in the Rain" in Passaic, and "Sugaree" in the Palladium, but this was the ultimate. "Sugar Magnolia," was the last dance of the blazing set. All four songs on my wish list became reality. The Grateful Dead played 2,314 shows during their enigmatic career, and this was the only time that "Shakedown," "Terrapin," "Dew" and "Sugar Magnolia" appeared in the same show. My friends, this was no coincidence. Grateful Destiny was calling me, and I accepted the charges.

Returning home from Philly, Seymour's little white Honda Civic struck a patch of ice on the Palisades Parkway, and the car went a-spinning towards some Rockland County pine trees. Luckily, the snow banks on the parkway median halted our spiral towards tragedy a few feet from the imposing pines. The little white Honda had to be pried loose from the snow by a tow truck. This was one of the longest days of my life, and it easily was the most thrilling—affirmation that I was on the right path—on the golden road to unlimited devotion.

Three days later, with Doug Schmell on the passenger side, I tore up the New York State Thruway in the maroon Chevy Caprice Classic that I'd inherited from my father. Our destination was Rochester, for another Grateful Dead extravaganza. The show was satisfyingly workmanlike, and after resting at a fellow Deadhead's crash pad, Doug and I sped south on Route 81 beneath brilliant early morning sunshine. Glancing at the clouds, I spotted an enormous pair of antlers attached to what appeared to be a statue of a rather large deer on top of a hill. Suddenly, the statue sprang to life and dashed towards the highway. I slammed on my brakes to avoid a collision, but Bambi was on a kamikaze mission. The reckless mammal looked right at us at the moment of impact, and then it careened off the front of the Chevy, wobbling through the air like a shanked punt on a windy day on Soldiers Field. The final result was a dead deer, and an almost totaled car, which I somehow managed to rattle all the way back to Nanuet, a 180-mile excursion. Astonishingly, I had escaped injury or death again. In spite of the fact that my friends and I weren't wearing seat belts in either auto incident, we paid no physical price—not a scratch, scrape, bruise, welt, or contusion marked our young bodies, and personally speaking, there were no mental scars. These incidents became instant folklore, amazing tales from my suddenly amazing life.

Worshiping music had always been an all-consuming passion, but now, I was an active participant in that process—a traveling witness in an underground counterculture circus, following, promoting, and hollering encouragement for the Great Garcia, and I had the finest traveling companion a Deadhead could imagine. Doug Schmell loved and propagated Garcia's music with purer enthusiasm than anyone I'd ever met. A master in the art of persuasion, Doug had the smile and charisma of a politician on the rise, the exuberant tone of a top flight play by play announcer, and the kid was terribly clever. He found outrageous ironies in the most commonplace circumstances. Doug carried himself with humble swagger. If you can envision an athletic Jim Morrison being raised by a middle-class Jewish family in the suburban comfort of Spring Valley, New York, then you get the picture. Doug could have easily drifted into any social scene in high school or college, but inspired by J. Garcia, Doug chose the long and winding road of weirdness into the underbelly of the American Dream. Mr. Schmell channeled all his charming conviction and robust optimism into his unofficial role as Garcia's Propaganda Minister.

Late on the sweltering afternoon of June 16, 1982, Doug and I began our journey to Music Mountain in his mama's yellow Cadillac Coupe de Ville, the car of choice for Jewish housewives in suburbia. We blazed north on the Palisades Parkway, which merged into Route 6, and after a quick jaunt over Bear Mountain, we segued onto 17 West, which took us right into the heart of the Catskills. A safe, leisurely drive was impossible with Doug behind the wheel. Grateful Dead raged from the speakers as Doug darted from lane to lane, tailgating numerous drivers at slightly excessive speeds. There was no malice in Doug's approach to driving, although those drivers who had a big yellow Caddy riding their bumpers might dispute that observation. Doug was a competitor, and life was his highway. Making good time was essential, even though we had all the time in the world.

As we exited Route 17 and headed towards South Fallsburg, I was engrossed with the sights of Sullivan county, and the contradictory extremes of her terrain. On one hand, the lush meadows, forests, and mountains glistened green, and the reservoirs sparkled beneath azure skies perfectly painted with cotton-candy clouds. On the other hand, this breathtaking aesthetic was scarred by maximum security prisons, poverty shacks, and forsaken hotels and bungalow colonies. This was a land of abandoned dreams that had seen better days.

Fifteen miles west of South Fallsburg lies Bethel, home to Woodstock, the festival that defined a time and place in American history. After passing by the modest Hassidic and African American enclaves of South Fallsburg, we spotted signs of hippie life; Deadheads milling around local grocery stores. As we closed in on Music Mountain, we spotted a group of naked freaks plunging into a nearby pond as if it were White Lake 1969 revisited. At last, some of that Woodstock Magic! The makeshift parking field buzzed as we arrived in the big ol' yellow Coupe DeVille and found a resting place alongside the rusty, banged-up vans, wagons, buggies, and cars of Deadhead Nation. This was a common scene at Grateful Dead shows, but not at JGB shows, which primarily took place in small, big-city venues. Since Bobby & the Midnites were performing after Garcia, and Billy Kreutzmann was playing drums for JGB, this was a family affair, a Deadhead gathering of the vibes. This would also be the largest outpouring of freak power this area had seen since three days of peace and music passed slowly through town in a four-day traffic nightmare.

Earlier in *Positively Garcia* I detailed the splendor of the Music Mountain performance, so I'll skip hitting you over the head with the same hammer, as much as we both might enjoy it. Before I joined the festivities on Music Mountain, I dropped a hit of window pane acid. My brain instantly conjured strange thoughts, interrupting my natural groove with Garcia. It wasn't anything approaching a bad trip, but I wished I'd never taken the plunge. I had a similar negative experience with mushrooms when I saw the Grateful Dead in Glen Falls on 4-14-82. After the show, I found myself at a party enjoying a few Molson Ales and a fresh tape of the show I'd just seen. The performances of "Jack Straw," "Deep Elem Blues," "Supplication," and "China Cat Sunflower" were stunning. I was there, standing on my tenth row seat, but where the hell was I? For geniuses like Hunter, Garcia, and Kesey, psychedelic experiences triggered breakthroughs in consciousness— the magic's ever-present in their works. I didn't need to fry my mind with acid to transcend with their art. I bid farewell to potent psyche-delics after Music Mountain. However, I remained faithful to other forms of debauchery.

After JGB finished their set, a driving rainstorm pounded the Catskills. Doug and I maintained our muddy turf for a substantial por-tion of the Bobby & the Midnites show, and then bailed in the nick of time. The parking lot became a swamp, and multiple vehicles were help-lessly ensconced in mud. Thanks to the power of the yellow Coupe, we were out of there swiftly, cranking Jerry on Route 17 and eagerly antici-pating the following night with JGB in New Haven.

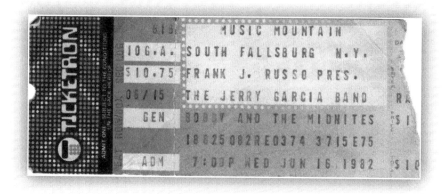

In the aftermath of the Rochester deer incident, my Chevy Caprice was running better than ever, thanks to reconstructive surgery at Manny's Auto Body Repair on Jerome Avenue in the South Bronx. I picked up Doug at the Schmell residence on Topaz Court in Spring Valley and drove towards New Haven. June 17, 1982, was Doug's nineticth birthday, and we were both in the early stages of the strangest years of our lives. This was my first jaunt to New Haven, which was only an hour away from Nanuet. My drive up the Connecticut Turnpike was like sweet and sour chicken: a mile between exits, sweet; twenty-five cent tolls every ten minutes, sour.

Weir opened for Garcia in New Haven, as they continued to alternate who'd play first, although JGB was the attraction de jour on this mini-tour. My amphetamine-fueled heart palpitated to the "Sugaree" opener. Garcia established an aggressive tone from the intro; each jam must be extended. There was a dramatic charge to the second solo, but Garcia held back just enough so that he could bring the house down with the finale. Brilliantly balancing emotion and execution, Garcia again treated Connecticut to a monster "Sugaree." In my heightened state of alertness, I shuffled and howled like a cockeyed lunatic. It was a fabulous, full-bodied "Sugaree," almost an immortal version. One song into the show, I scaled the mountain and danced in the Promised Land.

Music Mountain was the better overall performance, but there were no sloppy seconds in New Haven. "Sugaree" was followed by salacious versions of "Second That Emotion" and "They Love Each Other." The scorcher of the night was "Valerie," the new *Run For the Roses* blues tune that I barely knew. Locked in on Jerry and his Tiger from my twentieth-row seat in the left mezzanine, I was mesmerized by the primal sounds streaming from his guitar. When Garcia blows you away with a "Sugaree" or "Morning Dew," you expect it. When a jam comes out of the blue and stings you, it's something you never forget. This "Valerie" jam had that unshakeable effect.

After a one-set JGB affair was in the books, Weir came out with his bandmates Billy Cobham and Bobby Cochrane for a double encore. The first offering, "Man Smart, Woman Smarter," is a Harry Belafonte number that Weir began to overplay on Grateful Dead tours, and I loathed it almost instantly. The song appeals to the masses, and it especially arouses feelings of empowerment amongst the ladies. This is groovy and all, but the song always struck me as very gimmicky, unlike the band's venerated cover of "Aiko Aiko" which had a similar tempo and chord progression. After a one and done JGB debut, the night ended with a bone-crunching "Deal."

A few weeks after New Haven, Doug used his persuasive charms to convince me to lead an expedition to Wisconsin for a pair of weekend Grateful Dead shows at Alpine Valley Music Theatre in Wisconsin. It was a formative road experience. I would always feel at home on the road; my ancestors must have been Viking explorers. At Alpine Valley on 8-7-82, The Boys opened with an unprecedented The Music Never Stopped > Sugaree > The Music Never Stopped loop. Those were my two favorite first-set songs. I once again had that wild feeling of accomplishment, as if my dedication, and my personal mojo, was influencing these events that seemed miraculous at the time—the more I poured into this magnificent obsession, the greater the rewards. My visions were lucid, my mission was certain, and my conclusion, I believed, was glorious.

On September 15, 1982, I drove eight hours, down to the Capital Center in Landover, Maryland for my first show of the Grateful Dead fall tour. I was rewarded with an astonishing Playing in the Band > Crazy Fingers opener, the first time that psychedelic combo kicked off a show.

Anything was possible as long as I continued to make these pilgrimages. I had a carload of crispy Deadheads to relive me on the drive home if I tired, but this was my maroon Chevy, and completing the drive was a badge of honor. Ten Marlboros, seven bootleg tapes, four cups of coffee, and three pieces of Roy Rogers' fried chicken later, I made it back to my parent's house. After a hearty breakfast and shower, and without sleep, I took off for work at Ramapo Seafood, where I spent the day unloading trucks filled with 100-pound boxes of frozen shrimp, and then hauled the frozen sea creatures into a freezer and stacked the boxes as echoes of Garcia's guitar bounced around my fried brain.

When I wasn't manning-up in the cooler, I was a part-time student at Rockland Community College, a notorious breeding ground for middle-class Deadheads. Every semester I passed the classes I liked, and dropped those requiring actual studying. My priorities on campus were playing hoops and ping-pong, and networking with other Deadheads. During an era when rock and roll was in the dumps, and America was engaged in a nuclear arms race with the Soviet Union, Haight-Ashbury culture and the sacred underground world of the Grateful Dead was irresistible.

On November 10, 1982, the world was stunned to learn that Soviet Premier Leonid Brezhnev had died. Who would now be the new man in power at the Kremlin? Would this transition intensify the Cold War and push the superpowers to the brink of Armageddon? Pondering the world's fate would have to wait, because on the day Brezhnev died, I was on my way to see JGB at Livingston Gymnasium in Piscataway, New Jersey. The sobriety of the short drive was memorable. The driver, Mike Krieger, a high school acquaintance, banned smoking in his car. This was unconscionable, for I was a smokestack. The idea of going thirty-five minutes without lighting up a bone or a Marlboro was ludicrous. These were times when men and women smoked everywhere; in cars, on airplanes, in arenas and stadiums, and I even had a few professors who let students smoke in class.

I weathered my first smoking ban and then chain-smoked my way into Livingston Gymnasium. This was a small-time venue, as inauspicious as they come. It reminded me of the junior high school gymnasium where I went to my first dance. I had a great time shuffling around to JGB, yet the show made no lasting impression on me. Decades later I heard the boot of this show and it was kind of dull. It was as if Garcia was asking, "Why's a sweetheart like me playing in a dump like this?"

Back in the limelight again the following night, Garcia played an early and late show at the Felt Forum in the shadows of Madison Square Garden. The Grateful Dead had a riveting four-night stand at the Felt Forum in December of 1971. Pigpen was still wheeling and dealing, and the band was showing off many of their amazing new compositions, which would wind up on *Europe '72*. On 11-11-82, legendary New Orleans pianist Dr. John opened up both shows, but it might as well have been Dr, Ruth, I only had eyes and ears for JGB. I drove down to the 11-11-82 show with Mitch Rizzo. Rizzo was another high school chum who had recently discovered the joys of JGB.

As the early show got rolling, Rizzo mildly complained of chest pains. Rizzo dosed himself before the show, and I believed he was just suffering them old acid paranoid blues. This JGB lineup featuring Greg Errico on drums played with an aggressive East Coast attitude. The all-out assault they laid on the set ending "Sugaree" and "Tangled Up in Blue" had many hearts skipping a beat. There wasn't a shabby seat in the Felt Forum, and the acoustics were perfect.

At times these Felt Forum shows raged; at other times, Garcia sounded fatigued, and a little under the weather as he dutifully scrambled to keep up with the terrific tempo of the band. During "Harder They Come," Rizzo complained of chest pains again, and he suggested that he might need medical attention, or some fresh air at the very least. As someone who had retired from the mind-twisting effects of acid, I tried to convince him that everything would be all right, that these pains were manufactured by his worried mind. All this was taking place as JGB was burning down the house. After failing to reassure Rizzo with reason, and missing huge chunks of "Don't Let Go" and "Mystery Train," I had to compassionately rid myself of Rizzo. I promptly handed him over to a couple of cops standing by an exit door, telling them that good old Rizzo wasn't feeling well, and he needed to get some air and possibly some medical attention. With my conscience fully clear, I was dancing and jamming air guitar like a madman during "Deal." After a few minutes of big city air and noise pollution, the NYPD graciously let Rizzo back in for the "Midnight Moonlight" encore. I see Rizzo here and there every couple of years, and he always enjoys needling me about that incident, about how I handed him over to the cops and went back to see Jerry. What was I supposed to do?

JGB wrapped up their touring year at Wilkins Theater in Kean College on 11-15-82. My expectations of the venue were subdued after the Livingston Gymnasium show. Perry and I made the jaunt to Kean, and were thrilled by the inviting intimacy of the lush theatre. In fact, it seemed like a mistake. I half-expected the lights would go out and suddenly the cast from *Hello Dolly* would merrily frolic upon the stage. Well, it was merry, as Jerry kicked off the jubilee with "Sugaree." It felt like I was breaking some kind of code of conduct as I hollered and carried on, but before the night was over, Deadheads would turn this virginal venue into a den of debauchery. Garcia's voice struggled; perhaps it was laryngitis, or just the rigors of another year on the road—one too many mornings and a 1,000 miles behind. The shows were concise, yet the song selection was divine, especially the first four tunes of set two: "Mission in the Rain," "Harder They Come," "It Ain't No Use," and "Mystery Train." And come to think of it, Wilkins Theatre may not be the best name for a venue. When I hear that I think of John Wilkes Booth and the assassination of Abe Lincoln in a theatre.

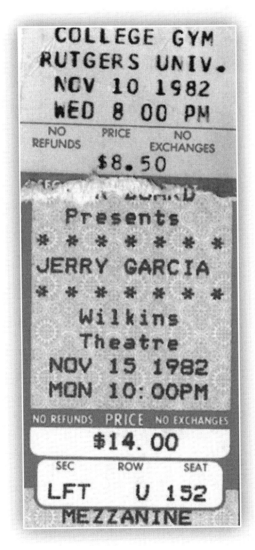

The demarcation point of my life was 1982. During my first eighteen years, I placidly protested my middle-class American experience. I didn't do homework, and I didn't aspire to getting A's. Being a Boy Scout never appealed to me; the uniform was a major turnoff. Although I enjoyed athletic competition, I had no desire to join a league or be part of a team, and once again, there's my issue with uniforms. I despised Halloween, and didn't trust religion. I believed in the world of AM and

FM radio, album covers, record sleeves, and 45s. I believed in protest songs, folk ballads, sappy ballads, prog rock, and rock operas. I believed in Beale Street, Bourbon Street and Broadway. I believed in the Beatles, Herb Albert, Herbie Hancock, CSN&Y, ELO, ELP, Jethro Tull, Pink Floyd and Jeff Beck. Thanks to the Grateful Dead, I wandered into an odd wheel of existence that embellished what I believed in. There were no rules, regulations, or restrictions. There were uniforms, but wearing a tie-dye was optional.

16

TANGLED UP IN JGB

Polka dancing in the Bushnell...romance and redemption at the Roseland...fear and loathing in Passaic...tough traveling on the Taconic... dash to the doors in Upper Darby...keeping the myth alive...

During a savage eight-day stretch in the spring of 1983, I saw ten Jerry Garcia Band shows. After rocking past the midnight hour, my companions and I drove back home every night. I was a twenty-year-old squatter in my folks' house, but they didn't seem to mind. Living on the road is hard traveling. Truckin' back to your parents' house after every gig is pure lunacy.

My descent into JGB madness began at the Bushnell Auditorium in Hartford, Connecticut on May 29. The following night, we were back at the Bushnell, courtesy of Doug's banana boat. We were joined by Bob the pirate, who was now known as "No Name Bob," a nickname he earned after he lent Doug a batch of sloppy boots: songs were misidentified, misspelled, and listed out of order, performance dates were incorrect, vague, or nonexistent. "No Name Bob" was born. His careless disregard for data mirrored his disheveled appearance.

The prospects seemed bleak for our ticketless trio. Saturday night, desperation and depression deepened around the Bushnell. There were no scalpers in sight—just Deadheads praying for the elusive miracle ticket. Suddenly, a door on the side of the theatre swung open. There stood a smiling freak, and behind him, a stairway to ecstasy. A bunch of us scampered up the carpeted steps like rats making a late-night raid on Taco Bell. Presto! We were dancing in the Bushnell balcony as Jerry whistled a "Mystery Train." Doug charged into a high-stepping, elbow-flapping polka dance. Nobody loves a "Mystery Train" bound for glory more than Doug. "No Name Bob" smirked in admiration, for he'd never had the pleasure of witnessing Doug under Jerry's spell.

The Bushnell shows whetted my appetite for the next tour destination—Jerry off-Broadway. Anticipation boiled inside the Roseland Ballroom. On the last day of May, New York City was juiced for a heaping dose of Garcia. Smoke billowed through the ballroom—that exotic, aromatic mix of hash, ganja and cigarettes. A huddled mass of hippies gathered close to the stage. The spacious ballroom floor was surrounded by carpeted walkways and lobbies and long, sleek bars from which there was a golden glimpse of the stage. Wherever one lingered or roamed, cocktail access was a cinch.

The Bearded One appeared on stage in a red T-shirt instead of his customary black—Summertime Santa. Garcia's belly expansion was obvious, bordering on obscene. He seemed to be adding ten pounds to his overburdened torso per tour. Melvin Seals, and the new backup singers Dee Dee Dickerson and Jacklyn La Branch were super-sized as well. This was a band that preferred a Grand Slam breakfast at Denny's over an aerobic session in Gold's Gym.

Jerry set sail with "Rhapsody in Red," its rhythm and chord structure similar to "Let It Rock," its slick jazz lick jutting free—*a deedle dee dee, a deedle dee diedle... a deedle dee dee, a deedle dee diedle.* Brightness vibrated from the furious jam, ideas exploding inside a rhythm and blues container. Fortified by funky organ-grinding, "They Love Each Other" playfully bounced in the second spot. Garcia ignited a two-tier jam: round one, a reconnaissance mission; round two, a searing solo that had the cosmopolitan hipsters howling their approval. Garcia was *en fuego*, and his boisterous devotees knew it. Matters of the heart ruled this set. Garcia blew the roof off the Roseland with diabolical fret work during "That's What Love Will Make You Do." The remainder of the gig was easy like Sunday morning, featuring a "Mississippi Moon" that made bikers weep. Jerry's tone was angelic:

"Honey, lay down bee-side meeeee; angels rock us to sleeeep."

I reconvened with Doug at the Roseland bar after the show. The NBA Finals flashed on a TV that dangled down by the single malt scotches. Doug's favorite athlete, Philadelphia 76ers Dr. J, was about to bury the Lakers. Dribbling near the right baseline, the Doctor charged to the basket and soared to the sky. Laker defenders guarded the hoop, forcing the airborne doctor behind the basket. Defying the laws of gravity and comprehension, Julius reappeared on the other side of the basket. And, with a casual flip of the wrist, the ball rolled from his fingertips, kissed the backboard and swished into the net—apple pie à la mode—impossible, but true. Philly had won the NBA Championship. Mere moments after "The Drive," a gaggle of security guards had to break up a ruckus between two lanky, but rather violent, hippies, and a few of their associates. The gladiators left behind a trail of blood. It was a grotesque conclusion to a righteous evening.

Back in the black T-shirt for night two of the Roseland rendezvous, Garcia crooned his mission statement: "I'll take a melody and see what I can do about it; I'll take a simple C to G and feel brand new about it." During "The Harder They Come," it felt like I was being checked into the boards of a hockey rink. The temperament of the performance reflected the international chaos of the times. Soviet-American tensions were peaking, Central America was a cauldron of revolution (who can ever forget the Sandinistas?), and the Middle East was the Middle East—no peace.

"Gomorrah," was an appropriate choice for a Hell's Kitchen dance floor brimming with whacked-out freaks gyrating to JGB—let the depravity and debauchery run wild. Neighborhoods west of the Roseland were being terrorized by sadistic Irish mobsters. The Westies instilled fear by ruthlessly chopping up their lifeless victims and stuffing them in Hefty® bags before depositing them in the East River. Pimps, hustlers, whores and dealers saturated Times Square, and squadrons of desperados loitered around the neon-lit sex shops. When Jerry sang, "Blew the city off the map, nothing left but fire," it sure sounded like prophecy. And, to some extent, it was. The West Side of Manhattan circa 1983 has been eviscerated. There's nothing left but clean-cut capitalism and grimy greed.

In the second half of the show, Garcia bullied four epic songs. If there was a gadget that could tally guitar notes played per minute, the device would have blown up. "Don't Let Go" featured a twenty-minute instrumental during which I chain-smoked three Marlboros. Gripping and terrifying, it was commensurate to navigating through turbulent oceans on a starless night. Edgar Allan Poe would have approved. *It was a dark and stormy night, wasn't it?*

The crowd rejoiced for "Dear Prudence." It came off as a tribute to Lennon because we were only two and a half years, and less than one mile, away from where John inhaled his last earthly breath. Garcia was the transformer, exploring layer after layer of a tune that's simply fetching, and quite strange in an elegant way. The solo was outstanding, landing just short of the great Cape Cod "Prudence" three nights earlier. "Deal" was a bloodbath! Garcia sang the song as if he was discarding a bag of chicken bones, but the jam was an act of acrimonious aggression. Garcia's notes swarmed like agitated hornets around the JackHammer bass and raging drums. When the set was over, it felt like the Roseland had been ransacked and simultaneously healed—a mass exorcism. With polarizing performances on successive nights, Jerry's mosaic art mirrored the passion and heat out on the streets of Manhattan.

Even the Lord needed a day of rest, and so did JGB and the nuts that followed them.

```
==  CAPITOL  THEATRE   ==  ==  PASSAIC  N.J.
  JOHN  SCHER  PRESENTS    DATE CODE     30 0RCH
THE  JERRY  GARCIA  BAND      10:30P       RGT
                                RGT  D    4
 NO  REF/EX  NO  CANS/BOTTLES                D
 04715098RE0245  0508E23      TAX  INCLUDED
 10:30P  FRI  JUN  03  1983    $12.50     4
```

The tour resumed in Passaic, New Jersey, on June 3, 1983. While I was sucking brew out of a pint in a seedy watering hole by the Capitol Theatre, a vaguely familiar face approached and asked me if I needed doses. I wasn't in the market, but Doug was. The freewheeling acid guy, who I think I knew from community college, looked like the Court Jester of Passaic, with his three-pronged joker hat and tie-dye sweatpants. He handed me a vial of LSD and instructed me to dose my buddy in the bathroom, $5 per drop. In the stall, I handed Doug the vial. He proceeded to dispense three or four drops on his outstretched tongue. Things were going to get real weird, real quick.

The healthy crimson hue vanished from Doug's mug. Beads of sweat rolled down his pale cheeks. Probing waves of the mega-dose zapped his brain and rattled his eyes. We fled the bar and stood on the street corner. Doug's arms and legs flailed wildly as he babbled gibberish. As nightfall descended upon Passaic, we had issues. How was I going to explain this to Herb Schmell? When Doug jumped into my Chevy that afternoon, theoretically, his future was bound for glory. The pride and joy of the Schmell clan, Doug was the heir apparent to his father's law practice. I had great respect for Herb and his wife Gloria. Though Herb never touched a drink or smoked, he had a zany wit and a fiery passion for life, which he had passed on to Doug. Herb also had a terrible temper; I could never explain to the old man why his son was being returned home a comatose vegetable, unfit to tie his own shoes.

My other concern was the nature of the environment we found our-selves in. Nighttime in Passaic was not conducive to psychotic episodes. What type of city was Passaic in the early '80s? The summer before, I'd pulled into Passaic for a JGB gig and found a spot a few blocks from the Capitol. Prior to parallel parking, I discharged Laurie and Tracy (the hippie goddesses of 11-10-81) from my maroon Caprice and told them to meet me in front of the Cap. A cop stopped the ladies, asked me to roll down my window and hollered, "What? Are you fuckin' nuts? Letting theeeese girls walk by themselves, in this neighborhood!? Are you fuckin' nuts?!? And if you don't move your car, you'll be lucky to have a fuckin' steering wheel left!"

So, there I was, on the hostile asphalt of Passaic, trying to find a sanctuary to nurse Doug back to sanity. I tried to lure Doug into the theatre, but his heart was pounding for the emergency room. After the ER doctor examined Doug, he assured us we had nothing to fear but fear itself. The good doc went back to treating emergency room causalities. We went to see the Captain.

There were two shows that night. We missed the early one and were tardy for the late show. My buddy proved to be a resilient son of a bitch. He was getting off on "Love in the Afternoon." Psychedelics stroked the sweet part of his brain as the calypso riffs rolled from Jerry's guitar. I was almost jealous. I'd twice missed my first live "Cats Under the Stars." What I missed was irrelevant. I was eternally thankful to be roll-ing up to the Schmell residence with their pride and joy intact.

Doug weathered the mega-dosing, and after a few hours of psychotic sleep, we were back on the trail of the Great Garcia. This time we were joined by my other primetime touring accomplice, Perry Paletta. I'd met Perry in tenth grade during my brief stint in Mr. Murphy's geometry class. Perry was a soft-spoken, blonde-haired Norwegian who wore a cappuc-cino-colored corduroy jacket and smoked Parliaments. We crossed paths again a few years later at Rockland Community College, and experi-enced our first Jerry shows together at the Capitol Theatre in '81. Perry was coming into his own as the lead guitarist of the Roadrunners. They played a whole lotta Dead and mixed in some Clapton, Hendrix, Dylan, Stevie Ray Vaughn, Little Feat, and CCR. They didn't have a distinctive voice at first, but inspired by Jerry, Perry's riffs and licks blossomed. The Roadrunners rapidly found their niche as a roadhouse jam band, becoming popular in the pubs and saloons of New City, Nanuet, Spring Valley, and Pearl River.

The day following his LSD meltdown, Doug was tearing north on the endlessly winding Taconic Parkway in his Coupe DeVille. I was riding shotgun, and Perry lounged in the back. When you're in the thick of a hedonistic marathon like this, the actual day of the week becomes meaningless. Still, it was Saturday night, and we were working our way back to JGB at The Chance in Poughkeepsie. As we drove through historic Poughkeepsie and admired the Hudson River to our west, I sensed the presence of Colonial America. I half expected to see Patrick Henry on horseback galloping through the cobblestone streets.

The Chance was a divine gathering nest for a JGB gig. Opened for business as the Dutchess Theatre in 1912, this red brick building resembled just about any old country barn and had a 900-person capacity. Closed from 1945–1970, it reopened as Frivolous Sal's Last Chance Saloon before officially being known as The Chance in 1980. The charming Chance was a tiny ballroom, theatre, and bar rolled into one. Such were the allures of a JGB tour. This front-porch atmosphere was unattainable at Grateful Dead shows.

With a long night and two shows ahead of us, Doug abstained from anything stronger than a few bong hits. He moved close to the stage and waited, anxiously, until the sweet twangs rang from Garcia's guitar. Perry and I met up with his older brother Stan and his friend Johnny Bell at the bar. With a can of Budweiser occupying one hand, I kept my other hand free to juggle joints, cigarettes, and bullets of blow. When the red velvet drape was raised, the band was already playing "Cats Under The Stars." Smiling wildly and wearing sunglasses, Garcia began to croon. A pleasantly pungent plume of marijuana smoke billowed through the Chance.

"Hey, Howie-baby!" shouted Stan. "Someone forgot to tell Jerry he's at the Chance. He still thinks he's at Coney Island, sunbathing." An eruption of laughter followed, and nobody chuckled harder than the messenger. Eight years older than Perry, Stan was built like a harpooner—broad, noble shoulders with a sloped stomach solid as granite. Grinning, Stan pivoted towards me and showed me how to wail air guitar left-handed.

With his knees slightly bent, Stan assumed a sturdy stance, arms opened wide, palms out, like a magician who had just plucked a rabbit from a bowl of chili. His expression turned serious as he peeked at his fingers as they slid across an imaginary fret board. Confidently strumming away with a bottle of Bud in his right hand, Stan was amused by his own antics. Suddenly turning towards his best pal, Johnny Bell, Stan the Man went through the same shtick all over again. Digging the groove all night long, Johnny Bell was a lumbering figure with thick brown hair compressed like a Brillo® pad. Although he had a bouncer's build, Johnny B. Goode had the goofy vibe of a Merry Prankster. Peeling twenties from his cash wad, Señor Bell financed our Budweiser pipeline. Johnny had recently picked the winning numbers in the New York State Lottery; however, he had the misfortune of having to share the $4,000,000 jackpot with six other winners. After taxes, his cut was about $20,000 a year for twenty years.

When the curtain was hoisted for the late show, JGB rocked "Rhapsody in Red." "Sugaree" was delightful to see; Garcia came off like a thousand turkeys gobbling in unison. Every show on this tour had its shining moments. The "Midnight Moonlight" encore had us prancing about like Russian Cossack dancers.

After partying with reckless abandon for the duration of two shows, Perry and I were sleeping soundly on the ride home as Doug drove drowsily south on the Taconic Parkway. We were all awoken by the screeching sound of steel scraping steel. Doug instinctively tugged the wheel to his left, steering us off the guard rail and separating us from a gruesome tragedy in

Hopewell Junction. Once again we'd danced with death. If it wasn't for a simple flick of the wrist, our Grateful odyssey would have been terminated.

There was a small dent on the yellow Coup de Ville—not the type of damage that would prevent Doug from driving to Upper Darby, Pennsylvania, for two shows at the Tower Theatre the following night. Enough was never enough—we had to keep on chasing lightning. A state trooper ticketed Doug for speeding on the New Jersey Turnpike. By the time we found the Tower Theatre and parked, we knew that the early show had begun. We sprinted a 100-yard dash to the theatre door in personal best times. For the third time on this tour we missed "Cats Under the Stars." I guess it just wasn't in the stars. JGB was wrapping up "They Love Each Other" as I caught my breath and strutted down the carpeted aisle. Garcia rewarded our tenacity with the only "Let It Rock" of the tour, a tremendous version with a pair of furious solos. That one "Let It Rock" made all the sacrifice worthwhile.

As for how Doug explained away the dent on the Coupe, I would find that out fifteen years later, at his wedding. During the best man's toast, Doug's younger brother, Eric, asked me to stand up and testify. In front of the entire Schmell clan, I was asked to swear that we actually hit a deer that night coming back from the Garcia show. I proceeded to perjure myself and kept the myth alive. Herb Schmell was laughing so hard his yarmulke almost dislodged from his head.

17

THE PRECIPICE OF
MADNESS

*Tour lag and its effects upon short and long term
memory loss...the donnybrook in Stony Brook...
JGB scheduling woes...more fear and loathing in
the Garden State...a late show for the ages...*

caught ten more JGB shows during the late fall '83 tour, although this
time, I spaced the dates out over a two-week period from November
30 through December 13. By year's end I was teetering on the precipice
of madness. In addition to my JGB jaunts, I rambled across America
to catch twenty-eight Grateful Dead gigs. My expeditions included
trips to Richmond, Greensboro, Hampton, Morgantown, Binghamton,
Providence, Worcester, Rochester, Harrisburg, Columbia (Maryland),
Philadelphia, East Rutherford, Hartford, New Haven, New York City,
Saratoga Springs, Lake Placid, Syracuse and Ventura, California.

It's odd how we can remember the minutia of events that happened
thirty years earlier. On the night of 11-30-83, I was knocking back brew
in a West Hartford bar with Perry, listening to Lionel Richie's megahit,
"All Night Long." Instead of singing along with Richie's chant of "Tam

bo li de say de moi ya/ Hey Jambo Jumbo," I improvised, "Sandinista government, Hey Sando Sando." Some worldly events did matriculate into my Garcia-dominated brain. As for that evening's performance, it's a great set list on paper, featuring, "The Way You Do the Things You Do," "When I Paint My Masterpiece," "It Ain't No Use," "Cats Under the Stars," "Rhapsody in Red," "Dear Prudence," and "Tangled Up in Blue." However, I don't remember a bloody note. I was suffering from tour lag, a condition that causes short and long-term memory loss if you don't give your head enough time to rejuvenate between tours. Another factor impairing my memory is that I've never acquired a boot of 11-30-83. It's the only JGB or Dead show I've attended that doesn't reside in my vast archive.

A few nights later, Doug and I were back on Garcia's trail, hunting for killer jams in the Gymnasium at SUNY Stony Brook, site of an eclectic Halloween Grateful Dead concert in 1970. The trip to Stony Brook was harrowing as we inched along the Long Island Expressway, motorist's hell on earth. We bided time with bowls of kind bud and hot boots, all the while praying that the Holy Spirit could guide us through the never-ending traffic stalemate before showtime. After parking on campus, we slammed the car doors and bolted towards the gym like Starsky and Hutch and joined the general admission festivities seconds before JGB claimed the stage.

Garcia didn't share our sense of urgency, as he promptly blew the opening line of "I'll Take a Melody." You've really got to be in a super-relaxed state to forget this line: "I've seen the rain falling down." That's like blowing "Oh, say can you see." Garcia's voice was shaky and ragged, a malady that had plagued him on this tour. The vocals of Jaclyn LaBranch and Dee Dee Dickerson were turned up louder than usual, but their contributions were a work in progress. Garcia relied on his guitar wizardry to save the day. As he picked, pecked, poked, and blazed his way through "Melody," the Deadheads in the gymnasium began folding up the chairs on the floor and stacking them in makeshift piles. The piles appeared like metal sculptures—improvisational homage from the inspired flock.

Garcia's soulful resiliency shined through on "The Way You Do the Things You Do." Blissful feeling burst through his comprised vocal chords, and the guitar solo smoldered and sizzled until it drifted back into the final chorus. In spite of Garcia's personal demons, he had an extremely impressive year performing with both the Grateful Dead and JGB. Yet, as I stood there in Stony Brook, I sensed Garcia was running on borrowed time. I had to savor these electric moments, which now seemed more heroic than ever.

No matter how muddled things seemed, Garcia had a knack for generating sensational theatre out of the blue. After kicking off the second set with "Mission in the Rain" and "Rhapsody in Red," JGB unloaded a medley of extraordinary songs beginning with an up-tempo "Don't Let Go" that was extremely catchy, and noticeably quicker than any version I'd ever heard. Instead of singing the final chorus of "Don't Let Go," the band segued the instrumental into "Deal," and then repeated that formula as they transitioned into "Tangled Up in Blue." Stringing these tunes together created an unforgettable collage—the donnybrook in Stony Brook—and it gave Garcia's ravaged voice extra recovery time. This type of JGB medley was as rare as a solar eclipse, and on this day, December 4, 1983, there *was* an actual solar eclipse!

After playing a pair of shows in Burlington, Vermont, and one in Amherst, Massachusetts, JGB returned to New York to make their debut at the Beacon Theatre on December 9. Taking full advantage of our welcoming Upper West Side surroundings, Perry and I loosened up for cocktails at the Bear Bar, a trashy watering hole two doors down from the glorious marquee of the Beacon Theatre. The curvaceous brunette bartenders were friendly and half-naked, the suds were dirt-cheap, and the jukebox pumped out Grateful Dead. I made a few trips to the besmirched men's room to relieve myself and powder my nose. I got hung up in the back with one of those basketball games, where for fifty cents you fire palm-sized red, white and blue balls in a six-foot-high hoop as rapidly as you can for sixty seconds. For a short Jewish kid with a ravenous smoking habit, I could still fill it up on any basketball court, simulated or real. After putting on a cocaine-frenzied display of marksmanship, I reconvened with Perry and the beauties behind the bar. Our loyalties were truly tested, but come 8:00 P.M., Perry and I bid farewell to the intoxicating debauchery and found our fourth-row seats next door.

Dressed to impress in black T-shirt and jeans, Garcia barreled into "Sugaree." The jams were rather fatty, much to my delight. Garcia's guitar playing was a tad sloppy and repetitive, but his drive and determination overwhelmed my snobbish critique. It was a heady early show featuring "Let it Rock" and "Someday Baby" in the middle. After all the traveling, struggling and striving, hearing fresh material was something to behold, and I was elated with my first "Someday Baby." The late show looked solid, but somehow it didn't affix itself to the recesses of my mind; it fell into that black hole of tour lag. I was at the following night's early and late shows at the Capitol Theatre. I've got the ticket stubs as proof, but my memories of that night are gone with the wind. Reviewing the tapes, I've concluded that these are exemplary fall '83 gigs—no reason to get excited.

After the Cap shows in Passaic, Garcia's posse traveled to Laker Hall in Oswego, site of the hallowed 2-17-80 rampage, for a gig the following night. Oswego is ten hours from Passaic, and Garcia's next show was back at Kean College in New Jersey two nights later. Who the hell scheduled this? New York and New Jersey are neighboring states, but one show is on the Great Lakes, and the other two were just off the Jersey Shore. A cranky Garcia dumped a five-song first set and three-song second set on Oswego—sentimentality be dammed!

I'm not sure how I found out about the 12-13-83 show at Kean College. There was no Internet or publicity machine touting these shows. But the word got out to those who needed to be there. I called up the Wilkins

Theatre on the morning of the show and learned that tickets were still available for both the early and late show. Perry wisely suggested that since it was only a half-hour drive from where we lived, that we should go down to Wilkins Theatre and procure tickets to this 953-seat venue before they were all snatched. And sure enough, we scored fourteen-dollar tickets to both shows. In the 1990s, JGB would have instantly sold out any show at Wilkins Theatre, and they could have easily fetched $150 a ticket.

Before the show, we met Doug inside the lobby of the Wilkins Theatre. Doug flipped some bud into a bowl, fired it up, and said, "Hey, Howie, you want a hit?" Uncharacteristically, I passed—chalk it up to tour lag—my weary brain was burnt to the bone. Doug hit on his pipe with nonchalant grace, as if he was in the cozy confines of his Albany dorm room. There was a Jersey cop staring him down, but this was the 1980s. Everybody smoked everywhere, especially in places where Jerry Garcia was doing his thing. However, this cop didn't adhere to this free-wheeling logic. In his mind, he saw a long-haired fiend brazenly smoking an illegal substance in the lobby of a college theatre, and promptly handcuffed and detained the suspect, who proclaimed his innocence all the way: "Come on, Officer. I'm a good guy. I was just minding my own business at a Jerry Garcia show. Please don't arrest me. I'm a decent guy, a pre-law student! Come on, Officer. You don't understand; I gotta see Jerry!"

Doug was carted away, and there wasn't a damn thing I could about it until the early show was over—more fear and loathing in the Garden State. I was giving Doug a ride home, so once again, I was responsible for returning him to the Schmell homestead. The early show was a little disappointing. Garcia was worse for wear after the excursion to Oswego. Perry and I visited Doug at a holding cell in the local police station between shows. I was relieved to tell him that the early show was a pile of cow dung. It was a sad, sad scene. There was something cruel and unjust in seeing the kid who loved Garcia's music more than anyone behind bars for a trivial transgression. Even sadder, we learned that law enforcement wasn't going to release Doug until later, meaning he'd miss the late show as well.

Back in Wilkins Theatre, JGB struck quickly with "Cats Under the Stars." In one swoop, this was more compelling than the early show. Fishing for a fantastic follow-up, Garcia reeled in "Catfish John." The Cats/Catfish combo was as rare as it was thrilling. The extended solos had that wonderful mixture of devotion and desire. On this final JGB show of the year, Garcia was hell-bent on playing a phenomenal show that would eviscerate the memory of any recent lackluster outings. Perry and I were giggling and giddy when Jerry jumped into "Someday Baby." All the other tunes we wanted materialized: "Rhapsody in Red," "Don't Let Go," "Tangled Up in Blue."

After Doug was released from the hoosegow, I had to gingerly tell him about the masterful performance. He was understandably distraught on the ride home, but no run-in with the law, automobile mishap, or bad trip could dim his burning zeal for Garcia. Around this time, Doug was graduating college and preparing for law school, yet these commitments were secondary to his obligation to spread the Gospel of Garcia. We spent the rest of the winter scouring all our sources for bootleg tapes and preparing for spring, which would yield a new cycle of Grateful Dead and JGB tours, and a bumper crop of tapes.

18

JGB UNDER THE STARS

Fresh air and fresh tunes for Jerry's Kids...Hey, Jerry,
where's the beef?...another immortal shrine bites
the dust...JGB endures a kamikaze hippie attack...
Garcia turns the heat up in Good Skates...

After years of secluded jamming in the smoky haze of gymnasiums, theatres, ballrooms, and clubs, JGB discovered Mother Nature on their Summer '84 East Coast Tour. Three of their first four gigs took place in the great outdoors. I was on hand for opening night at Philadelphia's Mann Music Theatre with my friend Scott Z. and his lady, Donna. Dancing and shuffling on the Great Lawn of the majestic amphitheater as the sun faded west, my body rejoiced as fresh air rushed into my lungs and the sweet vibrations of JGB consumed my head.

The opening set featured two tunes I'd never seen before. Garcia broke into a melody that sounded like "That's What Love Will Make You Do," but I was disappointed when I discovered it was "Get Out of My Life Woman," JGB's third live performance of Allen Toussaint's composition. Over the years I've developed an appreciation for "Get Out of My Life Woman," but at the time I hungered for familiarity. My other surprise was "Like a Road," an early Garcia/Saunders favorite that was returned to the rotation for tour '84. Garcia's matured voice cried out with the longing of any musician who had ever given fifteen consecutive years of his life to the road: "When the road gets too long/And you run all out of song/And the pain gets too much/For you to bear." This was a tear-jerker, as poignant as anything Garcia had ever sung, especially now in his obese Buddha-like state.

Three day later, Perry and I headed across Route 84 West for a show at Rocky Glen Amusement Park in Moosic, Pennsylvania. The sound of the venue had us salivating, as if this might be the sequel to Music Mountain—the numerical dates were balanced, all even numbers, 6-16-82 and 8-10-84. Rocky Glen turned out to be no Music Mountain, but we had a gay old time under the gigantic tent pounding brewskis with Perry's brother Stan, and Jonny Bell.

The moment tattooed to my mind occurred when Perry and I moved close to the stage during the "Tangled Up in Blue" encore. Jerry had ended the set with "Midnight Moonlight," but the hyped-up crowd chanted, "JERRY, JERRY, JERRY," till the big guy returned. About five yards away from Jerry, on his left-hand side, we were flabbergasted by the view. Garcia appeared like a pregnant grizzly bear roused out of hibernation. We were accustomed to Garcia's ever-expanding waistline, but this was nuts! Yet somehow, within this mass of flesh and clogged arteries burned a heart of gold which triumphed over the rules and regulations of human mortality. What a "Tangled Up in Blue!" Thanks to a Wendy's commercial, the catchphrase of the 1984 was "Where's the Beef?" Nobody had to ask that question at Rocky Glen Amusement Park. The beef was in the jam, as well as the man.

The following summer, Perry suggested an impromptu trip to see Bobby & the Midnites in Moosic, Pennsylvania. Usually we wouldn't travel an hour and a half to see Weir, but after JGB's performance, Rock Glen Amusement Park had become an immortal shrine. It's a good thing Perry was driving because I had a blinding migraine all the way to Moosic. The traffic into town was surprisingly slight, and the empty parking lot told us that something had gone wrong with our little scheme. Apparently Weir, and a gathering of freaks, had quite a hoedown under the tent the day before. Famished from the ill-fated journey, we stopped off at a local diner and were served by a waitress who had waited on the Great Garcia himself when JGB was in town. Somehow we took solace in that trivia. The evening wasn't a total bust; it was a pilgrimage of faith and fate. I doubt I'll ever have reason to return to Moosic. In 1987, Rocky Glen Amusement Park was closed—another shrine bites the dust.

The night after Moosic, JGB's next destination was an outdoor gig at Caldwell College. I traveled to this show solo, in my ol' reliable Chevy Caprice. Perry's band, which was now called The Lost Boys, was playing in a honky-tonk saloon in Nyack, New York, so I was looking at a Jerry > Perry doubleheader. It was a steamy night on the unpretentious Caldwell campus. A buzz of magnificence filled the air as the band shimmied into "Cats Under the Stars." There I gyrated, on a grassy knoll overlooking the stage, in a very '80s pair of skimpy black mesh shorts and a white T-shirt which pictured a gold skeleton floating on a raft and sipping from the straw of a potent cocktail. "Cats Under the Stars" was rapturous; it never had a longer or snazzier solo than it did on this night. I was in the midst of a memorable run: three shows in a row under the stars with JGB.

"They Love Each Other" bounced forth with boundless elation. Hissing sounds swished and swirled from Melvin's Hammond. Garcia's loaded solo slithered in tubular fashion as Kemper and Kahn framed it all into a beguiling package. Jacklyn LaBranch and Gloria Jones (new to JGB) complemented Jerry beautifully. This version is up there with the great Roseland versions of 5-31-83 and 6-1-83, and I knew that tomorrow, I'd be listening to a master audience recording of 8-11-84 on the second floor of the Schmell residence in Spring Valley. Doug turned his Garcia obsession up a notch in 1984 by becoming a taper. This was also the year when the Grateful Dead officially sanctioned taping of their shows by creating a taping section located behind the soundboards.

One of the unexpected highlights in Caldwell was the third number, the usually inconspicuous "Simple Twist of Fate." Garcia's guitar tone had a melancholy sparkle, and his growling of the final verse was more extreme than you or I would ever imagine. This performance digs deep, and it tugged on the hearts of everyone on hand. A pleasant "Run For the Roses" built the bridge to a stupendous "Dear Prudence" > "Rhapsody in Red" combo to end the set. Colossal! Hearing those songs back to back this early in a gig was unprecedented. This was the show of the year, bound for legendary status, until the whole kit and caboodle came crashing down, literally.

Following a "Mission in the Rain" second set opener, JGB rolled into "Get Out of My Life Woman." The band was hammering a nice groove until I heard a sudden thud, and a strange change in the sonic structure of the music. I noticed that part of the drum kit had been toppled over and a long-haired freak was being removed from the rubble. It was as astonishing as it was perplexing. A featherweight hippie, wired and whacked out of his tiny skull, had just climbed on the stage and bull-rushed right into the drums. The band continued to play, including Kemper, with whatever portion of his drum kit was still operational. From inspired to asinine, this was democracy and chaos hand in hand. Garcia was totally spooked, and who could blame him? Jerry tried to pacify the proceedings with "Like a Road," and then he split after a brief dash through "Midnight Moonlight." The idiotic act of one fool tainted the night; however, that first set is one of my most listened to JGB discs, a superb recording courtesy of D. Schmell.

If ever a JGB affair felt like a hometown show, it was the August 15 gig at Orange County Community College in Middletown. My father owned El Bandido, a Mexican restaurant in Middletown, and Orange bordered Rockland, where I was still taking classes at Rockland Community College. Up until this point it had been a typically hot August, but on this night the heat and humidity were barbaric. If there was any air-conditioning inside this field house, it was barely detectable. Outside of a sizzling "That's All Right Mama," this show was as flat as tapioca pudding. As rivulets of sweat rolled down Garcia, I only wanted the both of us to get out of there alive. It would have been fitting if Garcia sang, "Somebody help me, somebody help me...I have never been so lonesome and a long way from home."

An evening with Gerry Garcia of the GGB.

The JGB caravan rolled on to their next gig at a rink called Good Skates in East Setauket. For me and Doug, it was a two-hour drive, most of it on the congested Long Island Expressway. Ensconced in the lengthiness of the island, we passed Jericho, Commack, Hauppauge, Hicksville, Melville, and Terryville on our way to Jerryville.

Good Skates was as dumpy as any suburban roller-skating rink I may have frequented in my youth, yet there was always a buzz of great expectation in the air whenever Jerry played one of these arcane places. If the previous show in O.C.C.C. was like being in a sauna, Good Skates simulated being in a pizza oven. Although I was a good distance from the stage, I clearly noticed the perspiration flowing from Jerry's ashen skin. If there was ever a night in Jerry's career when he should have mailed in a short set, this was it. But on the last night of the tour, JGB withstood the condensed heat and played a show that would have thrilled a packed house in Madison Square Garden. During "Dear Prudence," I actually had to stop shuffling around because I was on the verge of collapse. Doug and I were hyped listening to the master boots on the way home. Garcia had a phenomenal night, and more phenomenal nights seemed inevitable. We believed our hearts and ears, not our eyes—the tantalizing allure of "Like A Road" and "Tangled Up in Blue" enabled us to escape from the obvious. We lusted for the next tour, but sadly, it would be three long years before JGB rolled east again, and by then, Garcia was a different performing artist.

19

ODE TO A SCI-FI BUFF

While working on this project, I emailed some JGB
questions to Ozzie Ahlers. Ozzie kindly recorded the answers
onto an audio file. These are the transcribed highlights
of that file. I wish I had the opportunity for a one-on-one
interview because I had a thousand follow-up questions in
mind. Regardless, this is a compelling reflection of Ahlers'
1980 stint as keyboardist for the Jerry Garcia Band.

HW: Tell us about how you became a member of the Jerry Garcia Band.

Ozzie Ahlers: Well, I was living in Marin County, and I'd been working with Van Morrison over a few years. I had been working with Jesse Colin Young, who was part of the fabric of that area of Northern California. And working with other people on and off, and I met up with Hunter doing a project. Bob Hunter asked me to come and record with him some, and I did, and got a big kick out of him; what a personality that guy is! And I did some touring with him. He had a band. I was asked to be the keyboard player.

I had already known John Kahn for some time. I got a call from Kahn, and he asked me about what was going on with Keith Godchaux, that he had had some problems, and would I consider being a part of Jerry's band. I said it sounds like a great idea to me. And Rock Scully gave me a call, filled me in on what was going to happen, and we went into rehearsals; that was about 1979. We started doing some local gigs and touring, and getting out to a couple of US East Coast tours, which you know about. And that's about the story of that one there.

HW: Were you familiar with the music of other JGB configurations before you joined the band?

Ozzie Ahlers: Well yes, I was. I certainly met Jerry through other folks along the way. Pete Rowan, an old friend of mine, was in a band called Seatrain with Lloyd Baskin. Lloyd's an old friend of mine, a great keyboard player, a great singer. He introduced me to Pete.
Pete and I stayed in touch over the years. Pete had told me that he was working with Jerry Garcia in Old & in the Way; he just said he was having a blast with it. And he told me about a guy named John Kahn, and all these different folks who played with him out there, and it sounded like fun. I was living and recording in Woodstock, and Paul Butterfield was putting a band together. He brought some people back from the West Coast—one of them was John Kahn—to audition for the gig. Another guy was Merl Saunders auditioning for the gig, and a lot of friends of mine from around there. But I was busy working on another project. I wasn't able to partake in any of that. But John started hanging out with us at some gigs that we were doing with local musicians who were playing in the area.

John Hall, a great guitar player for a band called Orleans; he and I were playing downtown. John came over and introduced me to Merl Saunders, who he told me he knew me through Pete Rowan. We went through the whole friendship thing and it really was great. Hall said, "Look, if you ever come to California, give me a call—here's my number," and Merl said the same. Well, that wasn't to be, because my next recording project was with this guy named Jackie Lomax up in Bearsville Studios. Jack was a friend of Van Morrison's, and Van happened to stop in. He was living there in Woodstock, and came by and asked me if I would consider being in his band, because he was moving to California. Well, I said yeah—the rest is history on that one. I moved out to California and hooked up with Kahn and Merl and my friend Marty David, who was playing in a bunch of bands. He had moved out from Woodstock also.

And those folks put me in touch with all the guys like Bill Vitt, Ron Starlings, and all those folks who sort of played in that area. Merl and I didn't get a chance to work much together. He was a keyboard player also. We touched base on some jams and stuff, but we never really played gigs together. What a wonderful guy he was.

So that's the story basically of getting my peek at what Jerry was doing, and all the people who he was working with, because by the time I got to California, these guys had all done gigs with Jerry. Merl, Kahn, Bill Vitt and Ron Starlings, they all had worked with him and said what a great guy he was.

HW: Where there any rehearsals. or was it just a trial by fire?

Ozzie Ahlers: Well, there were rehearsals. We'd go over to the big studio over on St. Francis Street, the Warehouse, and the historic Grateful Dead recording and rehearsal studios. And we would rehearse; we definitely would, especially with the four-piece (band). You want to have the idea of where we're going to go with the jams we were going to get into. But truthfully, we would play it any way we felt that night. And Jerry was an inspired player. If he felt like a song should be—if we should go to the bridge on a solo, he'd take it to the bridge. If he felt like the bridge wasn't necessary for the solo, we wouldn't do it. But we sort of knew each other well enough musically, and that was going to be the transcendental moment of however that happened.

Trial by fire, yes; it usually was on stage. You're going to allude to the "Eleanor Rigby" instrumental that came up; that's definitely Kahn. He's a jazz buff. Jazz and the blues buff, and he would love to do what the jazz guys did, and that would be bringing in a pop song and throwing it into the middle of a tune, and just allude to that for a while.

HW: Early in your first JGB tour, you guys flirted with "Eleanor Rigby" before it became a full-blown instrumental in the middle of "After Midnight." Was this jam discussed, or did it just naturally materialize as the tour progressed?

Ozzie Ahlers: There it is, the "Eleanor Rigby" instrumental in the middle of the "After Midnight." Yes, it was discussed. Yes, it was touched, because Jerry would play the line, John would fall in behind the line, and as a keyboard player, I might do the Beatles part. It didn't have a keyboard in it, because it was pretty much all string quartet, but we all went through the motions of it. It really became kind of exciting in the middle, and everybody dug it. It was a jazz moment. We all joked about how we were jazz players—we certainly weren't jazz players; we were rock and folk players. But we joked about how it was going to be done.

And then of course double time—that just happened. That was just like Jerry decided, sorry, I'm tired and waiting for these—da da da ba pa, ba da ba ba ba ba pa, (double time) da-da-da-da-duh, duh-da-da-da-duh-da-duh-da—he went right into the jazz tempo of it. So yeah, he was really cool. Let's see, we rehearsed that one and yeah, it became more apparent during the tour.

HW: The Kean College show is one of the most revered shows from your first tour with JGB. What are your recollections from that night?

Ozzie Ahlers: Well, I can tell you that that was a real fun tour. One of the great things about Jerry was that he liked to treat everybody well, and he paid everybody well. He was a very generous man, and really easy to work with.

And so when we got to the East Coast and we were going to do about four or five dates in one area, we'd set up shop in New York City, and that was a lot more fun than staying in Union, New Jersey and Providence, Rhode Island. Nothing against them or anything, but you would set up shop in New York City and take a limo out to the gigs in the case of Providence. And we had a private plane to take us to the longer hauls like Boston, and down to Atlanta. So yeah, it was really fun for me, especially since I'm from Summit, New Jersey, and Kean College is sort of—well, it was Kean College, and I think it's Kean University now. Most of those schools are grown up. And it was fun, because of course I saw people from my past; not just high school friends, but people I had met along the way. And being a musician, I played most continents of the world. And I have friends from all over, and they always end up on the East Coast of the United States. That's a great place to hear and see music; it's wonderful connecting with those folks.

So I do have a lot of great recollections of that gig in particular. Jerry had his kids, two of his girls along, and Carolyn, Mountain Girl, was sort of visiting. They were on good terms, because, well, he had two children with her. So they all came out to the gig and I got to see Annabelle and sort of, just sort of hang out with them, and it was a very nice gig for all of us.

The gig itself was inspired as usual. It was like, just another electric night, and we could have those electric nights anywhere, whether it was at the Keystone, or the Catalyst, or wherever it was that we played locally in California. We had some about 500- or 600-seaters where we'd just pack them asses to elbows in there and we'd jam and have fun. So yeah, we just brought that back to the East Coast and put it into theatres, and some arenas we played, always having fun with Jerry.

HW: What was it like improvising with Kahn and Garcia as a new member in the barebones JGB configuration?

Ozzie Ahlers: Well, we always jammed with Kahn and Pete Rowan on a bunch of things. We had a place called Lion's Share in San Anselmo, California, right at the crossroads, and everybody played there. When I was in Van Morrison's band, we'd show up—I mean, we'd be rehearsing with Van and we'd just say look, let's just go jam. We'd go down to the Lion's Share where the club owner would be glad to boot anybody off the stage and give Van a chance to play. And we jammed with each other. We'd jam with the musicians that were there, just kind of had fun. I mentioned Bill Vitt, who was also part of one of the JGB configurations, and we would just play, everybody would play. We had a saying about musicians. It might not be something you'd say as a compliment about somebody, but they'd say he has big ears, he or she has big ears. And they're referring to the fact that someone hears, which is sort of either before you get there, or just as you're going there and that someone goes with you, knows sort of musically inherently what's going to happen, and doesn't step all over you just because you usually do the bridge there. People who have big ears are able to hear that he is not setting up to the bridge, don't go to the bridge, stay in the verse. He wants to work it, he wants to work it. So that's what you do. You sort of listen to other players and yeah, I've been playing music since my first band when I was about 10 or 11 years old, so yeah. I have some experience in that.

HW: What are your lasting impressions of touring with Jerry Garcia?

Ozzie Ahlers: Well, this is a good part, because I can tell you about Jerry as one person, Jerry and Kahn together, as another person. Working with Rock Scully and having a standup guy like that around us, it was all just the way it should be musically, as far as I'm concerned. Touring, working with Jerry and knowing him outside the gig, I mean, he was going through some troubled times. When I was in the band, I'd go over and visit with him and John at a house they had in San Rafael, and there were some financial problems and other stuff going on.

Jerry was always kind and generous and no matter what, he split things with people. If you went to a gig, it was his name up on the board, Jerry Garcia Band, not the Ozzie Ahlers Band, not the John Kahn Band. But we'd walk away from that gig and we'd split it four ways, and I will tell you something—he was generous. In his will he left strict—I don't know how to say this—a strict testament that he wanted the money split equally with each band member, so if any projects came out under the JGB name, he would split the proceeds with everyone, and so even in his death he was able to keep that intact, and his family honored it. That's kind of how Jerry was. The other side of it (laughter); he was a sci-fi nut.

He and I had plenty to talk about on the tours. We both loved science fiction. We both really liked Frank Herbert, and especially the Isaac Asimov series, and a lot of the short stories and stuff like that. He wasn't impressed that I played with Van or that I did—my musical endeavors—that I worked in the south with Spooner Oldham and people like that who he really liked. Jerry was an R&B fan. He loved knowing that I worked with the people in Memphis.

But what Jerry was most impressed with was that I had met Isaac Asimov and that was (laughter) really big time to him. I told him in passing that I knew a gal in Woodstock, we were friends, her name was Tandy Sturgeon and her father was Theodore Sturgeon, a great science fiction writer. And I was invited over to the house for lunch to—I met her daddy, he was a very interesting guy. But he had a friend visiting there at the same lunch, and his name was Isaac Asimov, and I actually got a chance to sit and talk and have lunch with one of my idols in the science fiction world, and I think probably everybody's idol. He was sort of the grandfather of science fiction. If it wasn't Jules Verne, it was Isaac Asimov.

So Jerry had asked me over and over again, he would say, "So what did he say? What did he eat? I mean, did he eat salad?" He would ask me questions like that with those squinty eyes of his. Every once in a while he would go, "Man, I still can't believe you met Isaac Asimov!" And he would just say it in that funny way of Jerry's—only Jerry had that sense of humor. He and Kahn where almost like the humor twins. They had things that they would love to say to each other, and it always rubbed off on the whole tour and made it kind of a joyous time. So yeah, lasting impressions of Jerry: kind, generous, really experimental, and really creative and an enormous sci-fi buff.

Appendix

JERRY GARCIA BAND PERSONNEL 1975-1995

JGB #1
First show-September 18, 1975 Sophie's, Palo Alto
Last show-December 31, 1975 Keystone Berkeley
Jerry Garcia-guitar, vocals
Nicky Hopkins-piano, vocals
John Kahn-bass
Ron Tutt-drums
Gregg Errico-drums (December 31, 1975 Keystone Berkeley only)

JGB #2
First show-January 9, 1976 Sophie's, Palo Alto
Last show-January 10, 1976 Sophie's, Palo Alto
Jerry Garcia-guitar, vocals
James Booker-piano, organ, vocals
John Kahn-bass
Ron Tutt-drums

JGB #3
First show-January 26, 1976 Keystone Berkeley
Last show-August 12, 1977 Pier 31, San Francisco
Jerry Garcia-guitar, vocals
Donna Godchaux-vocals
Keith Godchaux-piano
John Kahn-bass
Ron Tutt-drums

JGB #3a
First show-July 8, 1977 Calderone Concert Hall, Hempstead, NY
Last show-July 9, 1977 Convention Hall, Asbury Park, NJ
Jerry Garcia-guitar, vocals
Keith Godchaux-piano
John Kahn-bass
Ron Tutt-drums, vocals

JGB #4
First show-November 15, 1977 Keystone Berkeley
Last show-November 3, 1978 Keystone Palo Alto
Jerry Garcia-guitar, vocals
Donna Godchaux-vocals
Maria Muldaur-vocals
Keith Godchaux-piano
John Kahn-bass
Buzz Buchanan-drums

RECONSTRUCTION
First show-January 30, 1979 Keystone Berkeley
Last show-September 22, 1979 Keystone Berkeley
Jerry Garcia-guitar, vocals
Ron Stallings-tenor sax, vocals
Ed Neumeister-trombone
Merl Saunders-organ, keyboards, vocals
John Kahn-bass
Gaylord Birch-drums
Notes: John Kahn had started Reconstruction as a contemporary jazz group, with the idea that Garcia would just be a guest. Shows were often billed as "Reconstruction with special guest Jerry Garcia."

JGB #5
First show-October 7, 1979 Keystone Berkeley
Last show-March 27, 1980 Keystone Berkeley
Jerry Garcia-guitar, vocals
Ozzie Ahlers-electric piano, synthesizer
John Kahn-bass
Johnny de Foncesca-drums

JGB #5a
First show-July 18, 1980 The Stone
Last show-August 9, 1980 Keystone Palo Alto
Jerry Garcia-guitar, vocals
Ozzie Ahlers-electric piano, synthesizer
John Kahn-bass
Gregg Errico-drums

JGB #6
First show-January 22, 1981 Keystone Palo Alto
Last show-January 23, 1981 Keystone Palo Alto
Jerry Garcia-guitar, vocals
Melvin Seals-organ
John Kahn-bass
Daoud Shaw-drums

JGB #6a
First show-January 27, 1981 Old Waldorf
Last show-June 1, 1981 The Stone
Jerry Garcia-guitar, vocals
Melvin Seals-organ
Jimmy Warren-electric piano

John Kahn-bass
Daoud Shaw-drums
Notes: Jimmy Warren joined the band on their third date at Garcia's request.

JGB #7
First show-June 25, 1981 Santa Cruz Civic Auditorium
Last show-June 26, 1981 Fox-Warfield
Jerry Garcia-guitar, vocals
Essra Mohawk-vocals
Liz Stires-vocals
Melvin Seals-organ
Jimmy Warren-electric piano
Phil Lesh-bass
Daoud Shaw-drums
Notes: Phil Lesh substituted for John Kahn for the debut of the vocalists.

JGB #7a
First show-July 23, 1981 The Stone
Last show-August 23, 1981 Keystone Palo Alto
Jerry Garcia-guitar, vocals
Essra Mohawk-vocals
Liz Stires-vocals
Melvin Seals-organ
Jimmy Warren-electric piano
John Kahn-bass
Phil Lesh-bass (August 22, 1981 Fairfax Pavilion only)
Daoud Shaw-drums

JGB #8
First show-September 7, 1981 Concord Pavilion
Last show-September 20, 1981 The Stone
Jerry Garcia-guitar, vocals

Julie Stafford-vocals
Liz Stires-vocals
Melvin Seals-organ
Jimmy Warren-electric piano
John Kahn-bass
Bill Kreutzmann-drums

JGB #8a
First show-October 25, 1981 Keystone Palo Alto
Last Show-November 20, 1981 Rainbow Theater, Denver, CO
Jerry Garcia-guitar, vocals
Julie Stafford-vocals
Liz Stires-vocals
Melvin Seals-organ
Jimmy Warren-electric piano
John Kahn-bass
Ron Tutt-drums

JGB #8b
First show-December 17, 1981 Keystone Palo Alto
Last show-June 22, 1982 The Mosque, Richmond, VA
Jerry Garcia-guitar, vocals
Julie Stafford-vocals
Liz Stires-vocals
Melvin Seals-organ
Jimmy Warren-electric piano
John Kahn-bass
Bill Kreutzmann-drums

JGB #8c
First show-June 23, 1982 Stanley Theater, Pittsburgh, PA
Last show-June 24, 1982 Capitol Theater, Passaic, NJ late show
Jerry Garcia-guitar, vocals

Julie Stafford-vocals
Melvin Seals-organ
Jimmy Warren-electric piano
John Kahn-bass
Bill Kreutzmann-drums

JGB #9
First show-October 13, 1982 The Catalyst
Last show-October 24, 1982 River Theater, Guerneville, CA
Jerry Garcia-guitar, vocals
Melvin Seals-organ
John Kahn-bass
Gregg Errico-drums

JGB #9a
First show-October 27, 1982 Rissmiller's, Reseda, CA
Last show-June 5, 1983 Tower Theater, Upper Darby, PA
Jerry Garcia-guitar, vocals
Dee Dee Dickerson-vocals
Jaclyn LaBranch-vocals
Melvin Seals-organ
John Kahn-bass
Gregg Errico-drums

JGB #10
First show-July 20, 1983 Keystone Palo Alto
Last show-July 24, 1983 Nevada County Fairgrounds, Grass Valley, CA
Jerry Garcia-guitar, vocals
Dee Dee Dickerson-vocals
Jaclyn LaBranch-vocals
Melvin Seals-organ
John Kahn-bass
David Kemper-drums

JGB #11
First show-September 30, 1983 Country Club, Reseda
Last show-November 19, 1993 Hampton Coliseum, Hampton, VA
Jerry Garcia-guitar, vocals
Gloria Jones-vocals
Jaclyn LaBranch-vocals
Melvin Seals-organ
John Kahn-bass
David Kemper-drums
(Gaylord Birch-drums: Oct 7 '85>Feb 2 '86 see JGB #12)

JGB #12
First show-October 7, 1985 Keystone Palo Alto
Last show-February 21, 1986 The Stone
Jerry Garcia-guitar, vocals
Gloria Jones-vocals
Jaclyn LaBranch-vocals
Melvin Seals-organ
John Kahn-bass
Gaylord Birch-drums

JGB #13
First show-February 4, 1994 The Warfield
Last show-April 23, 1995 The Warfield
Jerry Garcia-guitar, vocals
Gloria Jones-vocals
Jaclyn LaBranch-vocals
Melvin Seals-organ
John Kahn-bass
Don Baldwin-drums

Positively Garcia Setlists

1
Jerry Garcia and Merl Saunders
Sunday, Feb 6, 1972
Pacific High Recording Studio, San Francisco, CA

It Takes a Lot to Laugh, It Takes a Train to Cry
Expressway (To Your Heart)
That's a Touch I Like
Save Mother Earth >
Imagine
That's All Right, Mama
Who's Loving You Tonight
When I Paint My Masterpiece
I Was Made to Love Her
Lonely Avenue
How Sweet It Is

2
Jerry Garcia Band
Saturday, May 28, 1983
Cape Cod Coliseum, South Yarmouth, Massachusetts

- Set 1 -
How Sweet It Is
They Love Each Other
Knockin' On Heaven's Door
I Second That Emotion
Gomorrah
Run for the Roses

- Set 2 -
Rhapsody in Red
The Harder They Come
Don't Let Go
Dear Prudence >
Tangled Up in Blue
Encore: Midnight Moonlight

3

Jerry Garcia Band
Wednesday, Jun 16, 1982
Music Mountain, South Fallsburg, NY

- Set 1 -
How Sweet It Is
Catfish John
That's What Love Will Make You Do
Valerie
Let it Rock >
Deal

- Set 2 -
(I'm A) Road Runner
Love in the Afternoon
Don't Let Go
The Night They Drove Old Dixie Down
Run for the Roses

4

Jerry Garcia Band
Sunday, Feb 17, 1980
Laker Hall (State University of New York), Oswego, NY

- Set 1 -
I'll Take a Melody
Friend of the Devil
How Sweet It Is
Catfish John
Deal
Positively 4th Street
That's All Right, Mama

- Set 2 -
Money Honey
Sitting In Limbo
Let it Rock
After Midnight >
Eleanor Rigby Jam >
After Midnight
It Takes a Lot to Laugh, It Takes a Train to Cry
The Harder They Come

5
Legion of Mary
Friday, Jul 4, 1975
Great American Music Hall, San Francisco, CA

- Set 1 -
I Feel Like Dynamite
Someday Baby
That's All Right, Mama
Mississippi Moon
Boogie on Reggae Woman

- Set 2 -
Tough Mama
Little Sunflower
Tore Up Over You
Every Word You Say
My Problems Got Problems
It's Too Late
The Harder They Come

6
Jerry Garcia Band
Wednesday, Nov 4, 1981
Palace Theater, Albany, NY

- Set 1 -
How Sweet It Is
Catfish John
I Second That Emotion
Simple Twist of Fate
Mystery Train
Deal

- Set 2 -
(I'm A) Road Runner
Mission in the Rain
That's What Love Will Make You Do
The Night They Drove Old Dixie Down >
Tangled Up In Blue
Encore: Sugaree

7

Jerry Garcia Band
Tuesday, May 31, 1983
Roseland Ballroom, New York, NY

- Set 1 -
Rhapsody in Red
They Love Each Other
That's What Love Will Make You
Do
Valerie
How Sweet It Is
Run for the Roses

- Set 2 -
Harder They Come
Mission In The Rain
Mississippi Moon
Tangled Up In Blue
Gomorrah >
Deal
Encore: Midnight Moonlight

8

Jerry Garcia and John Kahn
Wednesday, May 5, 1982
Oregon State Penitentiary, Salem, OR

- Set 1 -
Deep Elem Blues
Friend of the Devil
Jack-A-Roe
Oh Babe, It Ain't No Lie
It Takes a Lot to Laugh, It Takes
a Train to Cry
Run for the Roses
Ripple
I've Been All Around This World
Valerie
Dire Wolf
Encore: Reuben and Cerise

9

Jerry Garcia Band
Thursday, Jul 24, 1980
Bushnell Auditorium, Hartford, CT

- Set 1 -
Sugaree
That's What Love Will Make You
Do
Friend Of The Devil
Simple Twist of Fate
Tangled Up in Blue

- Set 2 -
I'll Take a Melody
Sitting In Limbo
Russian Lullaby
Mystery Train
Mission in the Rain >
Midnight Moonlight

10

Jerry Garcia and Merl Saunders
Friday, Jun 30, 1972
Keystone Korner, San Francisco, CA

- Set 1 -
It Ain't No Use
Expressway (To Your Heart)
One Kind Favor
Sick And Tired
Biloxi
That's All Right, Mama
The Night They Drove Old Dixie
Down

- Set 2 -
It Takes a Lot to Laugh, It Takes a
Train to Cry
After Midnight
Money Honey
Are You Lonely For Me, Baby? >
Jam

11

Jerry Garcia Band
Tuesday, Dec 13, 1983
Wilkins Theatre (Kean College), Union, NJ
Late Show

- Set 1-
Cats Under the Stars
Catfish John
Someday Baby
Love in the Afternoon
Tangled Up in Blue

- Set 2 –
Rhapsody in Red
Gomorrah
Don't Let Go >
Midnight Moonlight

12

Jerry Garcia Band
Thursday, Feb 5, 1981
Stabler Arena (Lehigh University), Bethlehem, PA

- Set 1 -
How Sweet It Is
Catfish John
That's What Love Will Make You Do
Simple Twist of Fate
Let it Rock
Tangled Up in Blue

- Set 2 -
Sugaree
The Harder They Come
When I Paint My Masterpiece
The Night They Drove Old Dixie Down
Dear Prudence >
Midnight Moonlight

12 a

Jerry Garcia Band
Thursday, Aug 20, 1981
Keystone, Berkeley, CA

- Set 1 -
Sugaree
I Second That Emotion
Love in the Afternoon
Tough Mama
Mississippi Moon
(I'm A) Road Runner

- Set 2 -
Knockin' On Heaven's Door
The Way You Do the Things You Do
Don't Let Go
Lonesome and a Long Way From Home >
Dear Prudence >
Tangled Up in Blue

Howard Weiner's Dylan/ Dead road memoir, *Tangled Up in Tunes: Ballad of a Dylanhead*

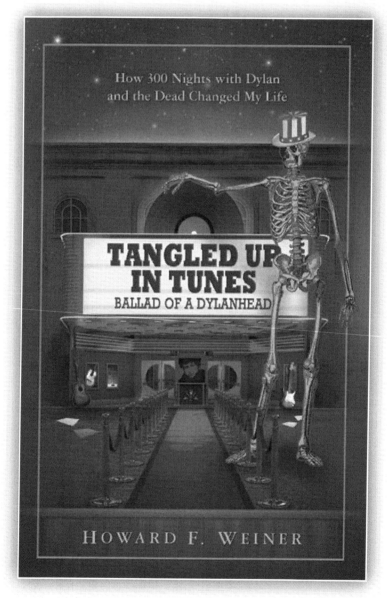

www.tangledupintunes.com

Made in the USA
Charleston, SC
07 July 2014